Bryan Stephens and Angela Buckingham

INTERNATIONAL EXPRESS

BEGINNER

Student's Book
with Pocket Book

OXFORD
UNIVERSITY PRESS

OXFORD
UNIVERSITY PRESS

Great Clarendon Street, Oxford, OX2 6DP, United Kingdom

Oxford University Press is a department of the University of Oxford.
It furthers the University's objective of excellence in research, scholarship,
and education by publishing worldwide. Oxford is a registered trade
mark of Oxford University Press in the UK and in certain other countries

© Oxford University Press 2013

The moral rights of the author have been asserted

First published in 2013

2020

10

No unauthorized photocopying

Links to third party websites are provided by Oxford in good faith and for
information only. Oxford disclaims any responsibility for the materials
contained in any third party website referenced in this work

ISBN: 978 0 19 457668 0

Printed in China

This book is printed on paper from certified and well-managed sources

ACKNOWLEDGEMENTS

*The publisher would like to thank the following for permission to reproduce
copyright photographs*: Action Plus p.86 (Vin Cox/ActionPlus); Alamy
Images pp.3 (Businesswoman drinking coffee/Paul Bradbury), 6 (Hispanic
businesswoman/Blend Images), 6 (portrait of man in mid fifties/Radius
Images), 6 (African couple hugging and smiling/Blend Images), 7 (crowd of
people/Ed Maynard), 16 (Japanese businesswoman/DAJ), 16 (Businesswoman/
Susan Vogel), 18 (Trinity Monastery Moscow/Gavin Hellier), 18 (Dubai United
Arab/Yadid Levy), 20 (Paul Bradbury/businesswoman talking), 19 (Happy
business couple/Andres Rodriguez), 25 (Portrait of young businesswoman/
amana images inc), 33 (Miami Skyline/Phil Degginger), 35 (Outline of a glass
of orange/Lannen Kelly), 35 (cup of tea/ICP), 35 (coffee/Lasse Kristensen),
35 (biscuits/Helen Sessions), 35 (Dundee cake/Keith Leighton), 36 (Blackberry/
Adrian Lyon), 36 (Mock gold card/RTimages), 36 (US passport/Greg Blomberg),
36 (First class boarding pass/Nicemonkey), 36 (Euro bank notes/Thomas
Klee), 37 (businessman/Denkou Images), 39 (man on mobile phone/Panorama
Productions I), 48 (London bus/Alan Moore), 48 (man in a car/Juice Images95),
48 (New your taxi on the road/Patrick Batchelder), 48 (boat/Christine Osborne),
48 (commuters crossing London Bridge/David Noton), 48 (easy jet plane/
DBURKE), 50 (V&A/Jack Sullivan), 51 (Spaghetti House restaurant/Jeffrey
Blackler), 51 (Hyde park in summer/Art Kowalsky), 51 (national gallery/
Alex Segre), 51 (Tourists in an open top bus/Anabell Lang), 54 (Mid adult
woman/amana images inc.), 54 (man standing by the metro/Radius Images),
55 (audience watching Bruce Hornsby/Visions of America), 56 (woman and
man next to a car/Stephen Ramsey), 56 (Raising the pole on Winston/Kos
Picture Source), 57 (Dubai Marina/Nico Tondini), 58 (Chicken Rendang Thai
curry/Andrew Twort), 58 (Croissant/Keith Leighton), 58 (Bowl of Spaghetti
with Tomato Sauce/Foodcollection), 58 (Three Fresh Oranges/ignazuri),
58 (WATERCRESS SOxford University Press/foodfolio), 58 (Baguette/Keith
Leighton), 58 (tiramisu cake/D. Hurst), 58 (Shish Kebabs/Fabrizio Troiani),
58 (Cous Cous/David Lee), 58 (salad/Keith Leighton), 58 (Bowl of rice/D. Hurst),
58 (Burger/Simon Belcher), 58 (Naan bread/Naan bread), 58 (Bunch of bananas/
Geoffrey Kidd), 58 (potato chips/blickwinkel), 59 (Union Jack/Tim Gainey),
63 (Yacht club, Dubai Marina/Jochen Tack), 64 (Two unpeeled cooked whole
prawns/Paul Springett 03), 66 (Doha airport/Juergen Stumpe), 66 (Qatar
airlines stewardess/Jack Sullivan), 71 (Flight attendant/Michael Moxter),
83 (Hotel luggage label/Amoret Tanner), 84 (bank card/Simon Margetson),
84 (Shower head/Jürgen Müller), 84 (Folded bath towel/Michele Constantini),
85 (Hotel reception/Greg Balfour Evans), 89 (Portrait of confident business
people/Yuri Arcurs), 97 (climbing a rock face/i love images), 98 (Brown Adidas
running shoes/Judith Collins), 98 (Sofas in Ikea furniture shop/Alex Segre),
98 (Hamburger/acestock), 98 (Macbook Air/Finnbarr Webster), 98 (Toyota
Verso-S/izmostock), 98 (Mobile Phone/Greg Balfour Evans), 98 (Handbag/Hugh
Threlfall), 98 (QANTAS Plane/Jo Katanigra), 102 (Man tying tie in mirror/),
107 (diners in a restaurant/Chris Ryan); Corbis pp.4 (Starbucks Cafe/LEX
VAN LIESHOUT), 5 (hands at computer), 6 (Businesswoman/HBSS), 9 (Woman
arriving at reception desk/Sean Justice), 15 (Co-workers talking/Ed Snowshoe),
16 (Portrait of a businessman/Image Source), 26 (Office Desks/Francis Zera),
28 (Confident businesswoman/PhotoAlto), 36 (green folder/Jamie Grill),
38 (Venice's Carnival/Andrea Merola), 39 (Young Businesswoman/Blue Jean
Images), 40 (businessman looking in diary/I Love Images), 40 (Businesswoman
talking on phone/HBSS), 48 (bullet train/Ocean), 50 (Harvey Nichols/
James Winspear), 51 (Empire Cinema/Paul Hutley), 61 (Wholemeal risotto/
Lawton), 73 (Businesswoman Using Laptop/Steve Hix), 76 (Dancers Fred
and Adele Astaire/Hulton-Deutsch Collection), 77 (The Waldorf-Astoria/
CORBIS), 79 (Fullerton Bay Hotel/Lauryn Ishak), 96 (Businesswoman working/
Cheryl Clegg), 96 (Hong Kong skyline/Image source), 97 (man skiing/Paul C.
Gallaher), 97 (woman scuba diving/Radius Images), 99 (patterned wallpaper/
Peter Carlsson), 100 (woman and man shaking hands/Jose Luis Pelaez Inc),
105 (Man and woman shaking hands/Dave & Les Jacobs), 108 (Honshu Island/
Hemis); Getty Images pp.3 (Business people having meeting/Chicasso),
5 (Businesswoman on the train/Javier Larrea), 6 (villagers gather to collect
water/Mark Hannaford), 6 (A Saudi man/arabianEye), 6 (groom holding
lollipop/Emma Innocenti), 8 (Woman talking on phone/Jose Luis Pelaez),
10 (Business people shaking hands/Paul Bradbury), 15 (Businessmen/Shannon
Fagan), 16 (Young Arab woman/Yvette Cardozo), 16 (Portrait of a male doctor
smiling/Glow Images), 17 (Office/BLOOMimage), 25 (portrait of a man/Loop
Delay), 36 (Business card holder/ULTRA.F), 36 Two businesswomen in back
seat of car/Bounce), 37 (Businessman walking in airport/Emmanuel Faure),
43 Two business people in discussion/arabianEye), 46 (man on his laptop/
Iconica), 46 (Businesswoman on the train/Javier Larrea), 47 (Buildings in
Sao Paulo/Panoramic Images), 49 (Portrait woman/Anjan Hegde), 60 (Waiter
Serves Food to Couple/Nico Kai), 64 (raw meat/Teubner), 66 (Plane flying
in the clouds/Caroline Purser), 67 (Smiling airline pilot on airplane/
Jupiterimages), 76 (Sinatra At Piano/Hulton Archive/Stringer), 76 (Laurence
And Marilyn/Harry Kerr), 80 (Businesswoman checking into hotel/Michael
Goldman), 96 (Businesswoman with laptop/Image Source), 96 (Businessman
sitting on chair/Image Source), 97 (Businesswoman looking at camera/
Image Source), 98 (Fashion mannequins/Bloomberg), 100 (Businessman and
businesswoman/image source), 100 (Woman and man shaking hands/Zero
Creatives); iStockphoto pp.27 (New York City/blueclueblue), 98 (Gold Rolex/
Pidjoe), 98 (sparkling-mineral-water/Carol Gering), 99 (floral seamless pattern/
Oksancia), 99 (Nataliia Kucherenko/vector texture with flowers), cover
(internet/enot-poloskun); Oxford University Press pp.5 (Male Telephonist/
Digital Vision), 5 (Young executives talking/PhotoAlto), 6 (businessman
smiling/Photodisc), 6 (Woman smiling/Photodisc), 10 (Young executives
talking/PhotoAlto), 21 (Businessmen shaking hands/Ariel Skelley), 35 (coca
cola/WR Publishing), 36 (Present/Photodisc), 36 (Laptop/David Cook), 39 (Male
Telephonist/Digital Vision), 48 (Cyclists in Shanghai/JLImages), 49 (Boardroom
presentation/OJO Images), 51 (Harrods/Oxford University Press), 55 (pizza/
Martin Bennett), 55 (Tourists on Tower Bridge/David Ashley), 58 (ice cream/
Photodisc), 58 (noodles/Stockbyte), 58 (Pizza/Image 100), 59 (Flag of Europe/
Graphi-Ogre), 59 (American flag/Graphi-Ogre), 59 (China Flag/Graphi-Ogre),
59 (Indian Flag/Graphi-Ogre), 59 (Brazilian Flag/Graphi-Ogre), 59 (Japanese
Flag/Graphi-Ogre), 59 (Saudi Arabian Flag/Graphi-Ogre), 64 (Crab/Photodisc),
59 (Eiffel Tower/Image Source), 64 (Aubergine/Thinkstock), 64 (Onion/
Stockbyte), 64 (Packet of crisps/Oxford University Press), 84 (American
Passport/Photodisc), 103 (French Flag/Graphi-Ogre), 103 (Russian Flag/
Graphi-Ogre), 103 (Italy Flag/Graphi-Ogre), 103 (Spanish Flag/Graphi-Ogre),
103 (Argentina flag/Graphi-Ogre); Rex Features pp.76 (The Beatles/Rex
Features), 76 (London The Savoy Hotel/Associated Newspapers); SuperStock
pp.64 (Roast chicken/FoodCollection/SuperStock), 64 (Variety of nuts/Food and
Drink/SuperStock), 64 (Eggs/Food and Drink/SuperStock), 64 (Swiss Cheese/
Flirt/SuperStock), 100 (Business woman and Businessman shaking hands/Juice
Images/SuperStock).

Cover images by kind permission: Corbis: (woman/Per Winbladh), (bridge/Image
Source), (desk/Marnie Burkhart); Getty: (coffee cups/Ron Chapple/Taxi), (man/
OJO Images).

Illustrations by: Peter Bull: pp.6 (map), 86 (map), 88, 90, 91, 95, 104; Peters and
Zabransky pp.26 (plan and icons), 68, 70, 74 (icons); Mark Duffin: pp.4 (food),
8 (ephemera), 28 (work station), 30 (food), 34 (office items), 78 (ephemera);
Rob Hancock: pp.9 (alphabet/labels), 19 (clocks), 20 (business card), 24 (clocks),
93, 107 (menus); Ben Hasler/NB Illustration pp.13, 78 (interiors); Gavin Reece
pp.75, 94.

Welcome to *International Express*

Your guide to the Student's Book Pack

Here are the details of what is in the pack and how the various parts of the course work.

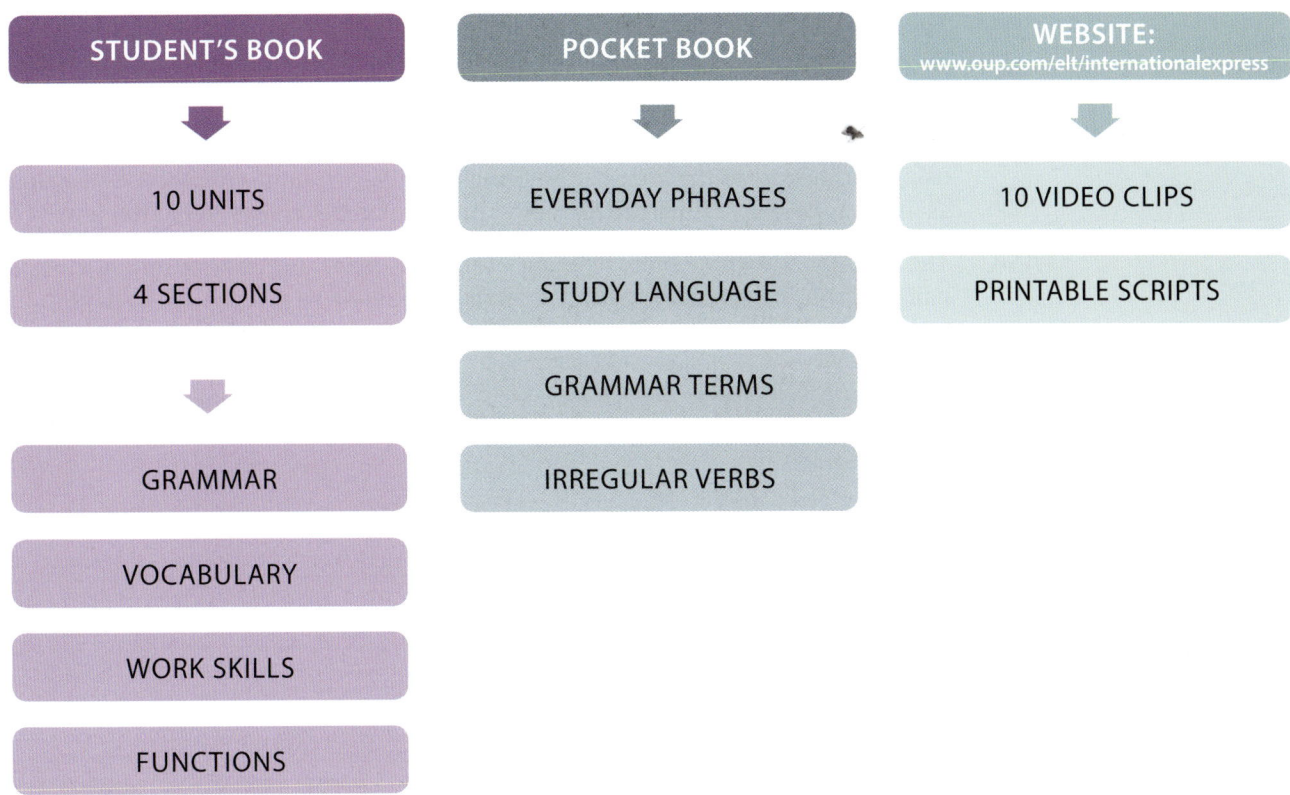

STUDENT'S BOOK	POCKET BOOK	WEBSITE: www.oup.com/elt/internationalexpress
10 UNITS	EVERYDAY PHRASES	10 VIDEO CLIPS
4 SECTIONS	STUDY LANGUAGE	PRINTABLE SCRIPTS
GRAMMAR	GRAMMAR TERMS	
VOCABULARY	IRREGULAR VERBS	
WORK SKILLS		
FUNCTIONS		

The **Student's Book Pack** contains the Student's Book and the Pocket Book.

The **Student's Book** has 10 units and each unit has four sections: Grammar, Vocabulary, Work skills, and Functions. One unit is six pages, and is followed by a Review section of four pages. The Review section can be done in class or for self-study.

The **Pocket Book** contains examples of everyday phrases taken from the Student's Book. This can be used at work or for travel to help remember and use key phrases. There is also a section on study language that gives examples of useful phrases for the classroom and expressions used in the Student's Book. *Grammar terms* has details about key words and phrases we use to talk about grammar. This is followed by a list of irregular verbs.

There is one video clip for every unit on the website. The topic of the video is linked to the topic of the unit.

How a unit works

The **Grammar** and **Functions** sections have four stages: Introduction, Focus, Practice, and Task.

INTRODUCTION

The language is introduced in a recorded conversation or in a reading text. There are questions to check understanding of the text.

FOCUS

The Focus highlights the main areas of the language introduced in the previous stage and asks some questions about how we form and use the language. The notes in the **Review** section help answer these questions.

PRACTICE

The Practice stage has activities to practise the language from the Introduction, using the answers to the Focus questions as a guide. The aim is to practise speaking as much as possible. There are further written practice exercises in the **Review**.

TASK

The section ends with a more open task to practise speaking and communicating in pairs or groups. More information about the tasks may be given at the back of the book in the **Task and activity notes**.

The **Vocabulary** and **Work skills** sections work in a similar way but have a more flexible format which allows for a variety of vocabulary and work skills to be studied and practised. There are further practice activities for both of these sections in the **Review**.

REVIEW
There is a **Review** at the end of each unit. It contains notes on the form and use of the language in the Grammar and Functions sections, and practice and review exercises for all four sections. There are listening, reading, and writing exercises which can be done as self-study or in class time.

TASK AND ACTIVITY NOTES
This section has notes for the tasks and activities in the unit. For some tasks, there are notes for Student A and Student B on different pages.

SCRIPTS
This section has all the scripts for the conversations and listening practice activities.

ANSWER KEY
The answers for activities and exercises in the units can be found here.

Contents

1 Pleased to meet you

Grammar *be: I, you, he, she, it, we, they*

INTRODUCTION

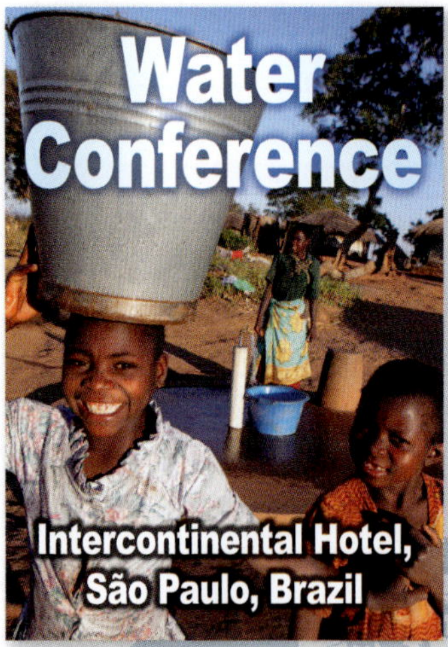

Water Conference
Intercontinental Hotel, São Paulo, Brazil

1 1.1 Listen and find the people on the map.

1 **A** Hello, I'm Adriana Gilberto.
B Hi, I'm Ken Scott.
A Welcome to the Water Conference.

2 **A** Hi. My name's Tim Brown.
B Hello. I'm Li Qin.
A Welcome to the Water Conference, Li Qin.

3 **A** Hi. I'm Aziz Mohamed.
B Hello. My name's Giovanni Fratelli.

4 **A** Hello. My name's Irina Ivanova. I'm from St Petersburg in Russia.
B Pleased to meet you, Irina. I'm Jean and this is Marie. We're from Saint-Louis in Senegal.

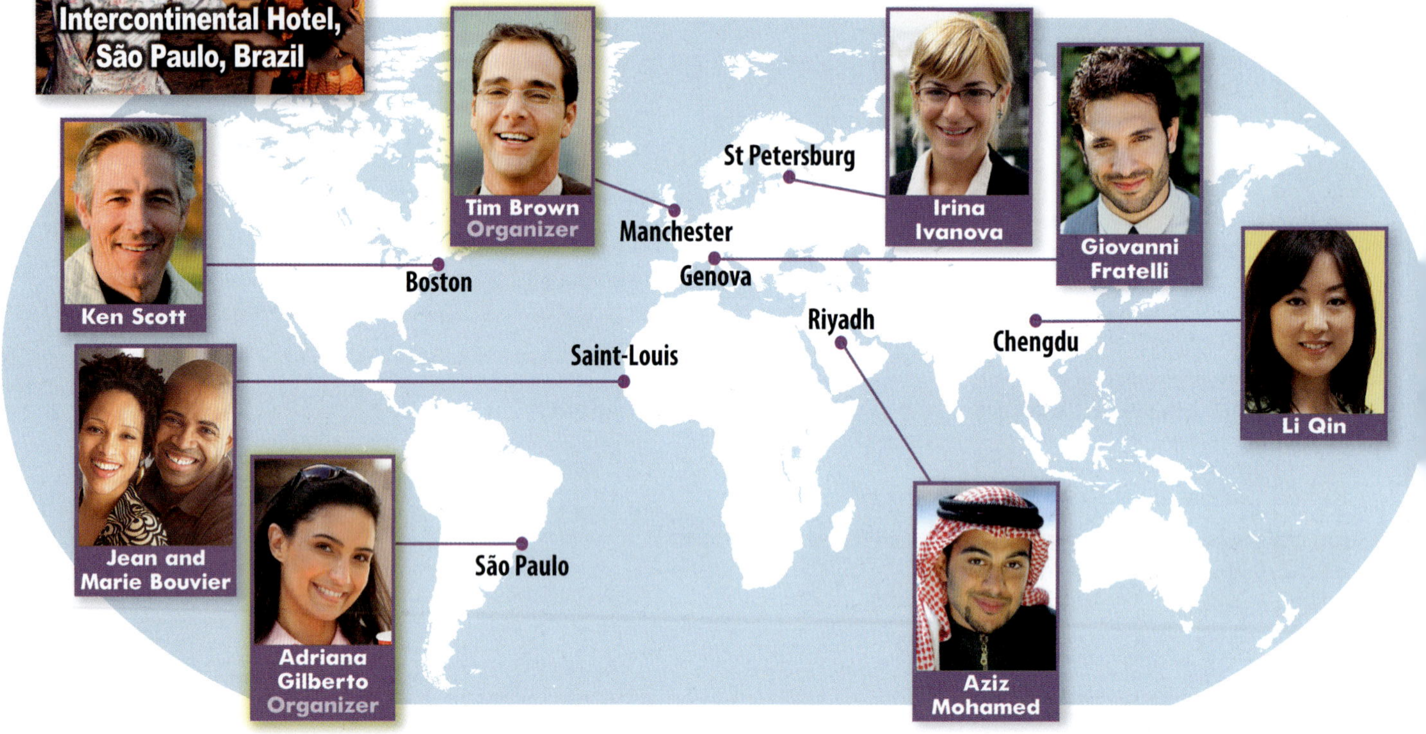

Tim Brown
Organizer
Manchester
St Petersburg
Irina Ivanova
Giovanni Fratelli
Ken Scott
Boston
Genova
Riyadh
Chengdu
Li Qin
Saint-Louis
Jean and Marie Bouvier
São Paulo
Adriana Gilberto
Organizer
Aziz Mohamed

2 Match the people with these countries.

USA UK Brazil China Russia Senegal Saudi Arabia Italy

3 1.2 Tim and Adriana check the people at the conference. Listen and complete the conversation with these words.

They're She's You're It's ~~He's~~

Tim OK. Let's check the people at the conference. This is Ken Scott.
Adriana That's right.
Tim *He's* ________¹ from Boston in the United States.
Adriana Yes. And this is Li Qin.
Tim Yes. ________² from Chengdu.
Adriana Chengdu?
Tim Yes. ________³ in China.
Adriana And this is Jean and Marie Bouvier. ________⁴ from Dakar in Senegal.
Tim Dakar? I think it's Saint-Louis.
Adriana Oh, yes. ________⁵ right. Saint-Louis.

Focus

Complete the table.

Long form	Short form	
I am	I'm	Giovanni Fratelli.
You are	_____	right.
He is	_____	from Saudi Arabia.
She _____	She's	from Brazil.
	It's	in the UK.
_____ _____		from China.
We are		
_____ _____	They're	from Senegal.

◉ **1.3 Listen and check your answers.**

Complete the rules.

We use *I* + _____ with our names.
Example I'm Adriana Gilberto.
We use *am / is / are* + _____ with our country.
Example We're from Senegal.

▸ For more details and practice, go to the Review section on pages 12 and 13.

PRACTICE

4 Complete the sentences.

1 A Hi, _____ Aziz. _____ from Riyadh in Saudi Arabia.
   B Hello, I'm Jean and this is Marie. _____ from Saint-Louis in Senegal.
2 A Is this Li Qin?
   B Yes. _____ from Chengdu in China.
3 A So _____ from Italy, Giovanni.
   B That's right. I'm from Genova.
4 A Is this Jean and Marie Bouvier?
   B Yes. _____ from Africa.
5 A Where's Boston?
   B _____ in the USA.
6 A Is this Tim?
   B Yes. _____ from Manchester in the UK.
   A And Adriana _____ from São Paulo in Brazil.
   B That's right.
7 A My name___ Irina Ivanova.

5 Work in pairs. Talk about people on the map.

Example A OK. This is Li Qin.
         B That's right.
         A And she's from China.
         B Yes, she's from Chengdu in China.

TASK

6 Meet people in your class.

Example A Hello, I'm _____. I'm from _____.
         B Hi. My name's _____. I'm from _____.

7 Introduce some people.

Example This is _____. She's from _____.
         This is _____. He's from _____.

Vocabulary Numbers 1–10

1 �))) **1.4** Listen and repeat the numbers.

0	1	2	3	4	5
_____	one	_____	_____	_____	_____

6	7	8	9	10
_____	_____	_____	_____	_____

2 Write the words under the numbers in **1**.

one   four   three   zero   ten   two   five   eight   seven   nine   six

3 Match the words 1–10 with the pictures a–j.

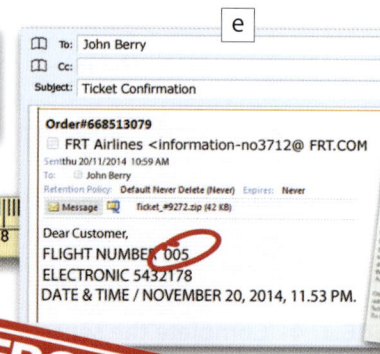

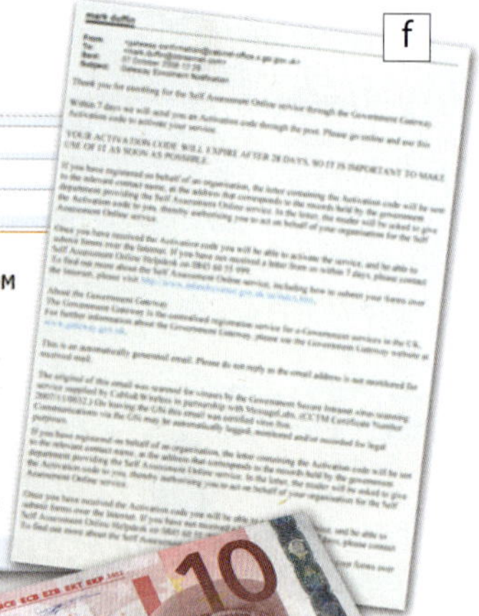

1	Flight zero zero five	___	6	Three days	___
2	Four business people	___	7	Terminal two	___
3	Room number seven	___	8	Six centimetres	___
4	One page	___	9	Ten euros	___
5	Nine nine nine	___	10	Eight degrees	___

4 ◍ **1.5** Look at the list of companies. Listen and write the building numbers.

Welcome to the Senate Business Centre

AlphaCo	7 ¹	Global	___ ⁴
Brand Link	___ ²	Hot Designs	___ ⁵
Casino Tec	___ ³	Nostrum	___ ⁶

5 ◍ **1.6** Listen to the voicemail messages at the business centre. Complete the telephone numbers.

1 Casino Tec   07963 4961*08*
2 AlphaCo   07762 7959___
3 Hot Designs   01865 3540___
4 Brand Link   07581 3955___
5 Nostrum   01865 9903___

6 ◍ **1.7** Listen. Repeat the telephone numbers.

7 Work in pairs. Read a telephone number from **5** and say the company name.

Example   A 07963 496108.
              B It's Casino Tec.

Work skills Spelling names

1 ◄)) 1.8 **Listen and repeat the alphabet.**

2 ◄)) 1.9 **Listen and circle the letters in 1.**

3 **Match the labels with the cities.**

1	Los Angeles	*LAX*	6	Mexico City
2	Amsterdam	_____	7	Lima
3	Berlin	_____	8	Miami
4	Cairo	_____	9	Caracas
5	Hong Kong	_____	10	Bangkok

4 ◄)) 1.10 **Listen and check your answers.**

5 **Work in pairs. Ask and answer questions.**

Example **A** What's M-E-X?
　　　　　B It's Mexico City … What's L-I-M?
　　　　　A It's Lima.

6 ◄)) 1.11 **Listen. Read the conversation.**

A Hello, I'm Kyra Tejero.
B Can you spell that, please?
A Yes. Kyra. K-Y-R-A.
B K-Y-R-A? Is that right?
A Yes. And Tejero: T-E-J-E-R-O.

7 ◄)) 1.12 **Listen and say the names.**

8 **Work in pairs. Meet and spell your names.**
Student A, go to page 106.
Student B, go to page 108.

Example **A** Hello, I'm Ajeet Singh.
　　　　　B Can you spell that, please?
　　　　　A Yes. Ajeet. A-J-E-E-T …

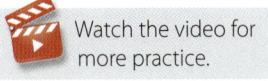 Watch the video for more practice.

Functions Introductions and greetings

1 ◉ **1.13** Angela Teo meets some visitors at her company. Read the list. Listen and tick ✓ the names of the people she meets.

Visitors	Tuesday 9.30				
Anne Rose	☐	Marvin Kantner	☐	Fernando Rodriguez	☐
Andy Rosser	☐	Lynne Murphy	☐	Fernando Ramirez	☐
Martin Katz	☐	Linda Morgan	☐		

2 ◉ **1.13** Listen again. Complete the conversations with these words.

Hello   I'm   This is   meet   Very nice   My name's

1 **Andy**   Good morning. _____ Andy Rosser.
   Angela   Good morning, Andy. My name's Angela. Angela Teo.
   Andy   Nice to _____ you, Angela.
   Angela   Nice to meet you too.

2 **Martin**   Hi. _____ Martin Katz.
   Angela   Pleased to meet you, Martin. I'm Angela Teo.
   Martin   Nice to meet you, Angela. _____ my colleague, Lynne Murphy.
   Angela   Pleased to meet you, Lynne.
   Lynne   Nice to meet you too, Angela.

3 **Angela**   Fernando Rodriguez?
   Fernando Yes.
   Angela   _____. I'm Angela Teo.
   Fernando Oh, Angela. _____ to meet you.
   Angela   Very nice to meet you too, Fernando.

3 Work in pairs. Read the conversations in **2**.

4 ◉ **1.14** Jess, Tariq, and Ross work together. Listen to them greeting each other in the office. Tick ✓ the phrases you hear.

1 Good morning. ☐   Pleased to meet you. ☐
   How are you? ☐   Great. ☐
   My name's Jess. ☐   Fine, thanks. ☐

2 Hi. ☐   Nice to meet you too. ☐
   How are things? ☐   Good. ☐
   Welcome. ☐   Pretty good. ☐

Focus

Complete the table with these phrases.

My name's Angela.   *Hi.*   *How are you?*   *Pleased to meet you.*
Good morning.   *Nice to meet you.*   *This is Andy Rosser.*   *Very nice to meet you.*
How are things?   *Hello.*   *Fine, thanks.*   *I'm Martin Katz.*

Introductions	Greeting friends and colleagues
My name's Angela.	

▶▶ For more details and practice, go to the Review section on pages 14 and 15.

PRACTICE

5 **Match the two parts of the conversations.**

1	Good afternoon.	a	Pleased to meet you too.
2	How are you?	b	And I'm Junko Yamamoto.
3	How are things?	c	Hello.
4	Good evening.	d	Nice to meet you, Jim.
5	Pleased to meet you.	e	Good afternoon.
6	I'm Peter Grant.	f	Fine, thanks.
7	This is my colleague, Jim Henson.	g	Good evening.
8	Hi.	h	Great.

6 **Order the conversation.**

Jane	Oh, good afternoon, Jia Li. I'm Jane Black.	___
Jia Li	Good afternoon. My name's Jia Li Woo.	*1*
Roy	And you. Welcome to the UK.	___
Jia Li	Pleased to meet you too, Roy.	___
Jia Li	Nice to meet you, Jane.	___
Jane	And you too. And this is my colleague, Roy Batty.	___

7 **Work in pairs. Practise the conversation in 6.**

TASK

8 **Introduce yourself to three students in the class.**

Example   A   Good _____. My name's _____.
             B   Good _____. I'm _____.
             A   Pleased _____.
             B   Nice _____ too.

9 **Now greet the same students.**

Example   A   Greet.
             B   Reply.
             A   How are _____?
             B   Reply.

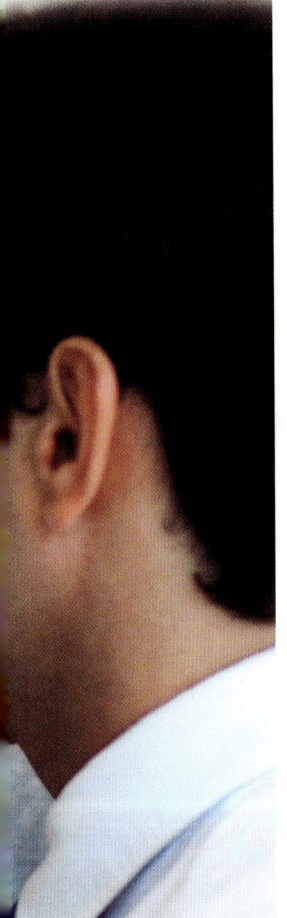

Review

Grammar *be: I, you, he, she, it, we, they*

Form

Long form	Short form	
I am	I'm	from Manchester.
You are	You're	welcome.
He is	He's	from Dubai.
She is	She's	from Saudi Arabia.
It is	It's	in Peru.
We are	We're	from the UK.
They are	They're	from France.
My name is	My name's	Pilar.

Use

We use *be* with our names.
Examples I'm Adriana Gilberto.
　　　　　She's Marie Bouvier.

We use *be + from* with our city or country.
Example We're from Senegal.

We use *be + in* with our city and country.
Example Chengdu is in China.

Short forms

We use the short form when we speak.
Example Hello, I'm Irina. (not 'I ~~am~~ Irina.')

PRACTICE

1 Write the long forms.

1 I'm from Russia.　　*I am from Russia.*
2 You're welcome.　　_____
3 He's Martin Katz.　　_____
4 It's in the UK.　　_____
5 We're from Medina.　　_____
6 They're from Saudi Arabia.　_____
7 My name's Mamdouh.　　_____

2 Complete the sentences with these words.

It's　They're　He's　I'm　We're　She's

1 Hello, *I'm* _____ Tim.
2 I'm Aziz and this is my colleague Mahmoud. _____ from Riyadh.
3 This is Li Qin. _____ from Chengdu. _____ in China.
4 This is Tim. _____ from Manchester in the UK.
5 This is Jean and Marie. _____ from Senegal.

3 Write complete sentences using the correct long form of *be*.

1 My name Dan. *My name is Dan.*
2 Where that? _____
3 He from Dubai. _____
4 What your name? _____
5 Where you from? _____
6 We from Saudi Arabia. _____
7 They from Argentina. _____

4 Complete the information for you.

1 My name is _____. I _____ from _____. It _____ in _____.
2 My English teacher is _____. _____ is from _____.
3 My mother is _____. _____ is from _____.

Vocabulary Numbers 1–10

1 Write the answers in words.

1 3 + 7 = *ten*
2 4 + 2 = _____
3 2 × 4 = _____
4 10 − 1 = _____
5 9 − 2 = _____
6 10 − 5 = _____

2 Write the numbers in the puzzle.

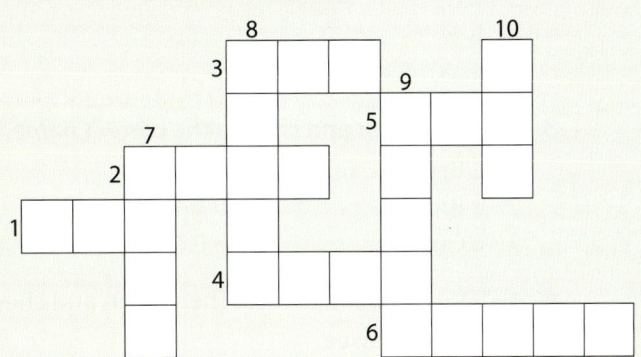

Clues

Across

1

2

3
(domino image)

4
3 × 3 =

5
(playing cards image)

6
6 + 2 =

Down

7
2 × 2 =

8
M68

9
Terminal 3

10
(bus image)

3 ◉ **1.15 Listen and correct the telephone numbers.**

1 020 6679 2143   _____
2 0113 901 8977   _____
3 (34) 94 719 0064   _____
4 (44) 1865 548332   _____
5 020 8813 0908   _____

Work skills Spelling names

1 ◉ **1.16 Listen to the sounds and write the missing letter.**

1 A H _ K
2 B C D _ G _ T V
3 F L M _ S X _
4 I _
5 O
6 Q _ W
7 R

2 ◉ **1.17 Listen and circle the odd one out.**

1 A B C D E
2 L O M F N
3 L H A K J
4 I E Y
5 T M E C G

3 ◉ **1.18 Listen and choose the correct name.**

1 a Bryan   b Brian
2 a Brown   b Brawn
3 a Connelly   b Connery

4 ◉ **1.19 Spell the names. Then listen and check.**

1 Barbara Losue
2 Anthony Eagle
3 Mahmoud Al Kouz
4 Mandy Rowland

Functions Introductions and greetings

We can make phrases with … *to meet you.*
Examples Nice to meet you.
Pleased to meet you.
Very nice to meet you.

We can make questions with *How …?*
Examples How are you?
How are things?
How's business?

We use different phrases when we meet people for the first time and when we greet people we know.

Introductions	Greeting friends and colleagues
Hi. Hello. Good morning / afternoon / evening. My name's Angela. I'm Jean Bouvier. Pleased to meet you. Nice to meet you. Very nice to meet you. This is Lynne Murphy.	Hi. Hello. Good morning / afternoon / evening. How are you? How are things? I'm fine / good / great.

We can use *Hi* and *Hello* for introductions and greetings.
We use greetings with *Good ...* at these times.
Good morning   before 12.00
Good afternoon   12.00 – 6.00
Good evening   after 6.00

PRACTICE

1 **Match the pairs. Mark *G* for greeting or *I* for introduction.**

1 Good morning.
2 Nice to meet you.
3 Hi.
4 My name's Juan Carlos Diaz.
5 How are you?

a Fine, thanks.   ___
b Nice to meet you too. ___
c Good morning.   G
d Hello.   ___
e Pleased to meet you, Juan Carlos. ___

2 **Complete the greeting conversation.**

Paul   Hi.
Karen   _____ ¹
Paul   How are you today?
Karen   _____ ²

3 **Complete the introduction conversation.**

Leo   Hi. My _____¹ Leo Chan.
Edward   Pleased to _____², Leo. I'm Edward Chu.
Leo   Nice to meet you, Edward. _____³ my colleague, Tina Leong.
Edward   Pleased to meet you, _____⁴.
Tina   Nice to meet you _____⁵, Edward.

4 **Match the conversations from 2 and 3 with photos A and B.**

Getting to know you

Grammar *be*: questions and negatives

INTRODUCTION

1 •)) **2.1 Adriana and Tim talk to people at the Water Conference. Listen and complete the profiles with this information.**

project manager   Dubai   Osaka   architect   designer   the Emirates

Surname	*Apaydin*
First name	*Mona*
Age	*28*
Country	_____ 1
City	_____ 2
Job	_____ 3
Married	*Yes*

Surname	*Aoki*
First name	*Toshihiko*
Age	*35*
Country	*Japan*
City	_____ 4
Job	_____ 5
Married	*Yes*

Surname	*Aoki*
First name	*Kimiko*
Age	*33*
Country	*Japan*
City	*Osaka*
Job	_____ 6
Married	*Yes*

2 •)) **2.2 Tim and Adriana check the details of two people. Listen and complete the profiles with this information.**

Spain   engineer   doctor   France

Surname	*Bonnier*
First name	*Yvette*
Age	*45*
Country	_____ 1
City	*Bordeaux*
Job	_____ 2
Married	*No*

Surname	*Gonzales*
First name	*Edmundo*
Age	*40*
Country	_____ 3
City	*Seville*
Job	_____ 4
Married	*No*

3 Look at the profiles. Choose the best answers.

1 Is Edmundo an architect?   a Yes, he is.   b No, he isn't.
2 Is Mona from the Emirates?   a Yes, she is.   b No, she isn't.
3 Are Toshihiko and Kimiko from Japan?   a Yes, they are.   b No, they're not.
4 Yvette, are you a doctor?   a Yes, I am.   b No, I'm not.
5 Toshihiko and Kimiko, are you married?   a Yes, we are.   b No, we're not.

Focus

Read the examples.

Question	Positive answer	Negative answer
Are you a manager?	Yes, I **am**.	No, I**'m not**.
Is she an architect?	Yes, she **is**.	No, she **isn't**.
Are you married?	Yes, we **are**.	No, we**'re not**.
Are they from Japan?	Yes, they **are**.	No, they**'re not**.

Complete the rules.

To make a question, we use _____ + *you*; _____ + *he, she, it*.
To make negatives, we use *I* + _____ + *not*; *he, she, it* + _____ + *not*;
you, we, they + _____ + *not*.

⏩ For more details and practice, go to the Review section on pages 22 and 23.

PRACTICE

4 Complete the conversations.

1
Adriana	Hello. _____¹ Adriana. _____ _____² Yvette Bonnier?
Yvette	Yes, _____ _____³.
Adriana	_____ _____⁴ from France, Yvette?
Yvette	Yes, _____ _____⁵.
Adriana	And _____ _____⁶ a teacher?
Yvette	No, _____ _____⁷. _____⁸ an engineer.

2
Adriana	_____ _____¹ from Tokyo?
Toshihiko	No, _____ _____². We're from Osaka.
Adriana	So, are you both engineers?
Kimiko	No, _____ _____³. I'm a project manager.
Toshihiko	And I'm a designer.

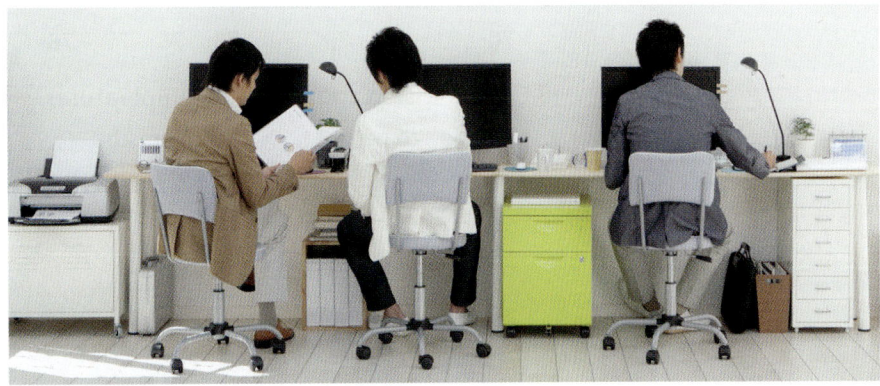

5 •)) **2.3** Listen and check your answers.

6 Work in pairs. Practise the conversations in **4**.

7 Work in pairs. Talk about people in **1** and **2**.

Example   A   Is Edmundo an engineer?
             B   No, he isn't. He's a doctor.

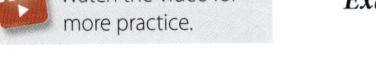
Watch the video for more practice.

TASK

8 Ask five students questions about countries and jobs.

Example   A   Are you from [country]?
             B   Yes, I am / No, I'm not. I'm from [country].
             A   Are you a/an [job]?
             B   Yes, I am / No, I'm not. I'm a/an [job].

9 Report back to your partner.

Example   A   (Pilar) is from _____. She's a/an _____.
             B   (Maria and Max) are from _____. They're _____.

Vocabulary Numbers 11–100

1 ◉ **2.4 Listen and repeat the numbers.**

11	12	13	14	15
eleven	_____	_____	_____	_____

16	17	18	19	20
_____	_____	_____	_____	_____

2 Write the words under the numbers in 1.

twelve   ~~eleven~~   eighteen   fourteen   sixteen
seventeen   nineteen   fifteen   twenty   thirteen

3 ◉ **2.5 Listen and repeat the numbers.**

20	30	40	50	60
_____	_____	_____	_____	_____

70	80	90	100
_____	_____	_____	_____

4 Write the words under the numbers in 3.

thirty   fifty   a hundred   ninety   seventy   forty   twenty   sixty   eighty

5 ◉ **2.6 Listen to the differences.**

1	13 thirteen	30 thirty	5	17 seventeen	70 seventy
2	14 fourteen	40 forty	6	18 eighteen	80 eighty
3	15 fifteen	50 fifty	7	19 nineteen	90 ninety
4	16 sixteen	60 sixty			

6 ◉ **2.7 Listen and <u>underline</u> the numbers you hear in 5.**

7 ◉ **2.8 Listen and repeat.**

70   71   72   73   74   75   76   77   78   79   80

8 ◉ **2.9 Listen and write the temperatures.**

1 Shanghai _____   4 Brasilia _____   7 Paris _____
2 Sydney _____   5 London _____   8 Mecca _____
3 Moscow _____   6 Dubai _____

9 Work in pairs. Talk about the temperature.

Example   A Is it cold in Shanghai?
　　　　　　　B No, it's eighteen degrees.

10 Work in pairs.

Student A Write five numbers from 1 to 100. Say them to your partner.
Student B Write the numbers you hear.

Work skills Talking about schedules

1 ◗) **2.10** Listen and repeat the times.

1 It's ten o'clock. 2 It's ten thirty. 3 It's ten forty-five. 4 It's eleven o'clock. 5 It's eleven fifteen.

2 Write the times.

1 _____ 2 _____ 3 _____ 4 _____ 5 _____

3 ◗) **2.11** Listen and check your answers.

4 ◗) **2.12** Look at the schedule. Listen to Adriana talk about Day 2 of the Water Conference. Complete the times.

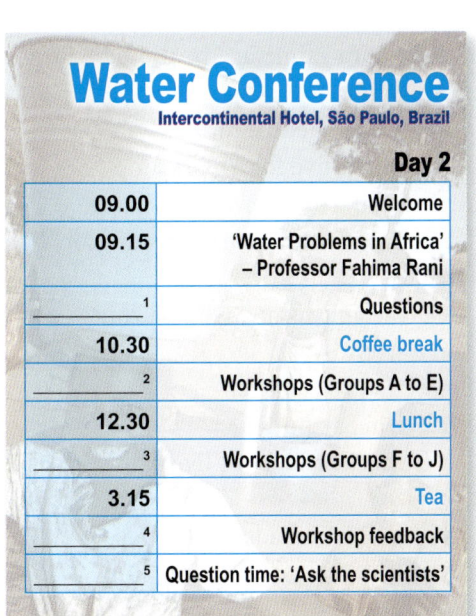

Water Conference
Intercontinental Hotel, São Paulo, Brazil

Day 2

09.00	Welcome
09.15	'Water Problems in Africa' – Professor Fahima Rani
_____ ¹	Questions
10.30	Coffee break
_____ ²	Workshops (Groups A to E)
12.30	Lunch
_____ ³	Workshops (Groups F to J)
3.15	Tea
_____ ⁴	Workshop feedback
_____ ⁵	Question time: 'Ask the scientists'

5 ◗) **2.13** Listen to the conversation.

A Excuse me. What time is the coffee break?
B At ten thirty.
A Thanks.
B You're welcome.

6 Work in pairs. Practise the conversation in **5**.

7 Work in pairs. Ask and answer questions about the schedule in **4**.

Functions Exchanging personal information

INTRODUCTION 1 ●)) 2.14 **Listen and read the conversation between Laura Zumeta and Volker Ziegert.**

Volker	Hello. My name's Volker. Volker Ziegert.
Laura	Hello, I'm Laura Zumeta. Are you here for the conference?
Volker	Yes, I'm a trainer.
Laura	Are you on the schedule today?
Volker	Yes, at one forty-five for a workshop.
Laura	Great! Are you from Germany, Volker?
Volker	No, I'm not. I'm from Austria. I work for Watertime …
Laura	Watertime?
Volker	Yes, it's a research company in Salzburg.
Laura	Are you a scientist?
Volker	No, I'm a project manager.
Laura	So, you live in Salzburg?
Volker	No, I'm from Austria, but I live and work in Lagos, in Nigeria.
Laura	Really?
Volker	Yes, it's great. I travel a lot too. I travel to Asia, Europe, and South America for my job. And you, Laura? …

2 **Look at the business card. Find two mistakes.**

Volker Ziegert
Scientist
Watertime Research Company
Salzburg, Nigeria

Office   + 670-11-43407100
Mobile   +3 901 234 5678
Email   ziegertv@watertimerc.aus

3 ●)) 2.15 **Read and complete the introduction. Listen and check.**

Laura	Eva, this is Volker Ziegert. He's from _____[1].
Eva	Nice to meet you, Volker. I'm Eva Gonzalez.
Volker	Nice to meet you too, Eva.
Laura	Volker works for _____[2]. He's a _____[3]. He lives and works in _____[4].
Eva	Really?
Laura	Eva is a teacher. She works for WTL. It's a charity. It's in Argentina, but she lives in Peru.
Volker	How interesting!

Focus

Choose the correct answer.

a	I'm …	(name) / job.
b	I'm a/an …	job / company.
c	He works in …	city / company.
d	I work for …	city / company.
e	It's a (research) …	country / company.
f	She lives in …	country / company.
g	I travel to …	country / company.

▶ For more details and practice, go to the Review section on page 25.

PRACTICE

4 Complete the sentences. Match 1–7 with a–g.

1 I'm …
2 I live in …
3 I work in …
4 I work for …
5 It's an …
6 I'm an …
7 I travel to …

a Asia for my job.
b Cairo.
c JCo Ltd.
d Egypt.
e Abdul Rachman.
f engineer.
g oil company.

5 ●)) 2.16 Listen and complete the conversation.

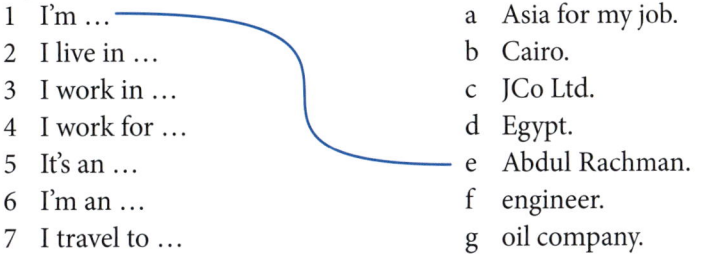
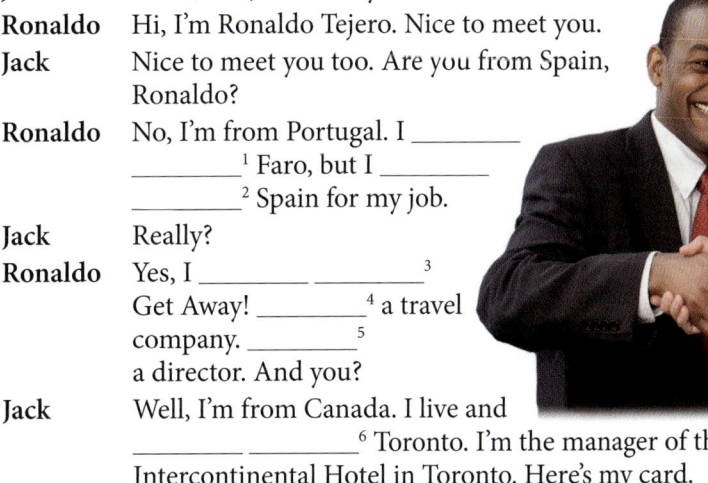

Jack Hello, I'm Jack Nutley.

Ronaldo Hi, I'm Ronaldo Tejero. Nice to meet you.

Jack Nice to meet you too. Are you from Spain, Ronaldo?

Ronaldo No, I'm from Portugal. I _____ _____[1] Faro, but I _____ _____[2] Spain for my job.

Jack Really?

Ronaldo Yes, I _____ _____[3] Get Away! _____[4] a travel company. _____[5] a director. And you?

Jack Well, I'm from Canada. I live and _____ _____[6] Toronto. I'm the manager of the Intercontinental Hotel in Toronto. Here's my card.

Ronaldo Thanks.

6 Work in pairs. Practise the conversation in **5**.

TASK

7 Work in pairs. Exchange personal information. Talk about:

- your name
- country and town
- company and job
- travel for work

Example **A** Introduce yourself: Hello. My name's …

B Reply and give your name. Ask where your partner is from: Are you from …?

8 Tell another student about your partner.

Example Serge is from France …

Review

Grammar *be*: questions and negatives

Form

Question			Positive short answer	Negative short answer
Are	you	from France?	Yes, I am.	No, I'm not.
Is	he	a doctor?	Yes, he is.	No, he isn't.
	she	an architect?	Yes, she is.	No, she isn't.
	it	in China?	Yes, it is.	No, it isn't.
Are	we	married?	Yes, we are.	No, we're not.
	you	from Chile?	Yes, we are.	No, we're not.
	they	engineers?	Yes, they are.	No, they're not.

We do not use the short form in positive answers.

Example   A   Are you a doctor?

              B   Yes, I am. (not 'Yes, ~~I'm.~~')

Negative

I	'm not / am not	a doctor.
You	're not / are not	a teacher.
He / She	isn't / is not	from Lima.
It	isn't / is not	in the Emirates.
We / You / They	're not / are not	from Dubai.

We can make short negatives in two different ways for *you*, *he/she/it*, *they*, and *we*:

You're not. / You aren't.   We're not. / We aren't.

He's not. / He isn't.   They're not. / They aren't.

●)) 2.17 **Listen and repeat the negatives.**

Use

We use *be* to ask and answer about names, jobs, and ages.

Examples   A   Are you Adriana Gilberto?   B   Yes, I am.

              A   Are you teachers?   B   Yes, we are.

              A   Is he 45?   B   Yes, he is.

We use *be* + *from* to ask and answer about cities or countries.

Example   A   Is she from New York?   B   No, she isn't.

We use *be* to ask and answer if someone is married.

Example   A   Are they married?   B   No, they're not.

Short and long negative forms

We use the short negative forms when we speak.

Example   I'm not from Spain.

We use the long negative forms when we write.

Example   He is not a doctor.

a and an

Form

I'm He's She's	a	doctor. manager. teacher.
	an	engineer. architect.

We use *an* before a job name starting with a vowel (a, e, i, o, u).
Example I'm an engineer.

We use *a* before a job name starting with other letters (consonants).
Example He's a teacher.

We do not use *a/an* with *we*, *they*, or *you* (plural).
Examples We're doctors.
They're architects.

Use

A and *an* are called articles. We use articles with job names to talk about the jobs we do.

PRACTICE

1 Make negative sentences.

1 He's from Dubai.   *He isn't / He's not from Dubai.*
2 She's a doctor.   _____
3 I'm an architect.   _____
4 They're from the United States. _____
5 We're married.   _____

2 Make questions (1–4). Match with the answers (a–d).

1 He's 35.   *Is he 35?*
2 They're engineers.   _____
3 You're from the USA.   _____
4 She's married.   _____

a Yes, she is.   ___
b No, they're not.   ___
c No, he isn't.   *1*
d Yes, we are.   ___

3 Choose *a*, *an*, or no article (–).

1 Are you *a /* (*an*) */ –* engineer?   4 Is he *a / an / –* manager?
2 She's *a / an / –* doctor.   5 I'm *a / an / –* architect.
3 We are *a / an / –* teachers.   6 Are they *a / an / –* engineers?

4 Answer the questions.

1 Are you from Europe?   _____
2 Are you a business person?   _____
3 Are you a student?   _____
4 Are you 30 years old?   _____
5 Are you single?   _____

Vocabulary Numbers 11–100

1 ◉ **2.18** Listen and circle the numbers you hear.

1 18 88 89 80
2 17 70 71 77
3 60 16 64 66
4 50 55 15 54
5 13 31 30 33
6 40 44 14 41

2 Write the answers in words.

1 10 + 1 = *eleven* _____
2 4 × 4 = _____
3 8 × 10 = _____
4 60 ÷ 4 = _____
5 46 − 7 = _____
6 twenty-two × three = _____
7 ninety-three ÷ three = _____
8 thirty-four − sixteen = _____

Work skills Talking about schedules

1 Write the times on the clocks.

1 six ten   2 six thirty   3 six forty   4 six forty-five   5 six twenty   6 six fifteen   7 six fifty

2 ◉ **2.19** Listen and repeat the times in **1**.

3 ◉ **2.20** Listen and complete the schedule.

Water Conference
Intercontinental Hotel, São Paulo, Brazil

	Day 3
09.00	Welcome
09.10	Workshops (Groups A to E)
ⁱ _____	Coffee break
² _____	Talk: 'Clean water for all' – Dr Fiona Hofer
³ _____	Lunch
2.30	Workshops (Groups F to J)
⁴ _____	Tea
4.40	Goodbyes

Functions Exchanging personal information

In business, we talk about our job, our company, our country, and city.

Examples   I am a doctor.
I work for Doctors Without Borders.
It's a non-government organization (an NGO).
I'm from Australia.
I live in Sydney.
I work in Africa.

We ask questions and make responses to show we are interested.

Example   A   Are you a doctor?
B   Yes, I am. I work for Doctors Without Borders.
A   Really? How interesting!
B   And you?

PRACTICE   **1**   ◉) 2.21   **Listen and complete the fact file about Satoko Yamamoto.**

Name: *Satoko Yamamoto*

Country: _____ [1]

Lives in: _____ [2]

Company: _____ [3], recruitment company

Job: Recruitment officer

Travels to: _____ [4]

2   **Write about Satoko Yamamoto. Use these words.**

lives in   is   works for   is from   is   travels to

<u>Satoko is from</u> _____

_____

_____

_____

_____

3   ◉) 2.22   **Listen and complete the fact file about Andreas Westermann.**

Name: *Andreas Westermann*

Country: _____ [1]

Lives in: _____ [2]

Company: _____ [3]

Job: _____ [4]

Travels to: _____ [5]

4   **Write about Andreas Westermann. Use these words.**

lives in   is   works for   is from   is   travels to

<u>Andreas</u> _____

_____

_____

_____

_____

3 | In the city

Grammar *there is, there are*

INTRODUCTION   **1** Read the MyOffice home page.

MyOffice · · · · · · · · · · · · · · ·

MyOffice finds the perfect office space for businesses. There are offices in the USA including New York, Chicago, Miami, San Francisco, and Dallas. There is also a branch of MyOffice in the UK. There are office spaces for small, medium, and large companies.

Find the perfect office space for your business.

How do I search?

Search by country

United Kingdom ⌄

Search by company size

Small ⌄

2 Complete the sentences about MyOffice. Tick ✓ the correct sentences.
1 MyOffice is   ☐ *a computer company*   ☐ *an office rental company.*
2 There are offices in   ☐ *New York* ☐ *Los Angeles.*
3 There is a MyOffice branch in   ☐ *the UK* ☐ *the Emirates.*

3 Match the room names with the rooms A–D in the office map.
reception ___   meeting room ___   offices ___   kitchen ___

Now match these places 1–8 with the icons a–h.
1 elevator ___   2 parking ___   3 internet connection ___   4 coffee shop ___
5 restaurants ___   6 shops ___   7 banks ___   8 train station ___

a ☕   b 🌐 www   c 🛗   d P   e 🛍   f 🚆   g X   h $

4 ●) **3.1** Listen to Yoon Kwon from GIIR and Rick Costa from MyOffice.
Tick ✓ the rooms and places they talk about in **3**.

5 Are the sentences true or false?

		True	False
1	There is a centre on Fifth Avenue.	☐	☐
2	There are two meeting rooms.	☐	☐
3	There are five offices.	☐	☐
4	There is a kitchen.	☐	☐
5	There isn't an internet connection.	☐	☐
6	There is an elevator.	☐	☐
7	There isn't a train station near the centre.	☐	☐
8	There aren't any banks near the centre.	☐	☐

Focus

Read the examples.

Positive	Negative
There is a reception.	**There isn't** a coffee shop.
There are five offices.	**There aren't** any banks near the centre.

Question	Positive answer	Negative answer
Is there a gym?	Yes, **there is.**	No, **there isn't.**
Are there any banks?	Yes, **there are.**	No, **there aren't.**

Complete the rules.

We use *there* + _____ with singular nouns and *there* + _____ with plural nouns.

We use _____ or _____ + *there* to make a question.

We use *there* + _____ or _____ to make a negative sentence.

▶▶ For more details and practice, go to the Review section on pages 32 and 33.

PRACTICE

6 Yoon Kwon talks to her director. Complete the sentences. Use the information in **4**.

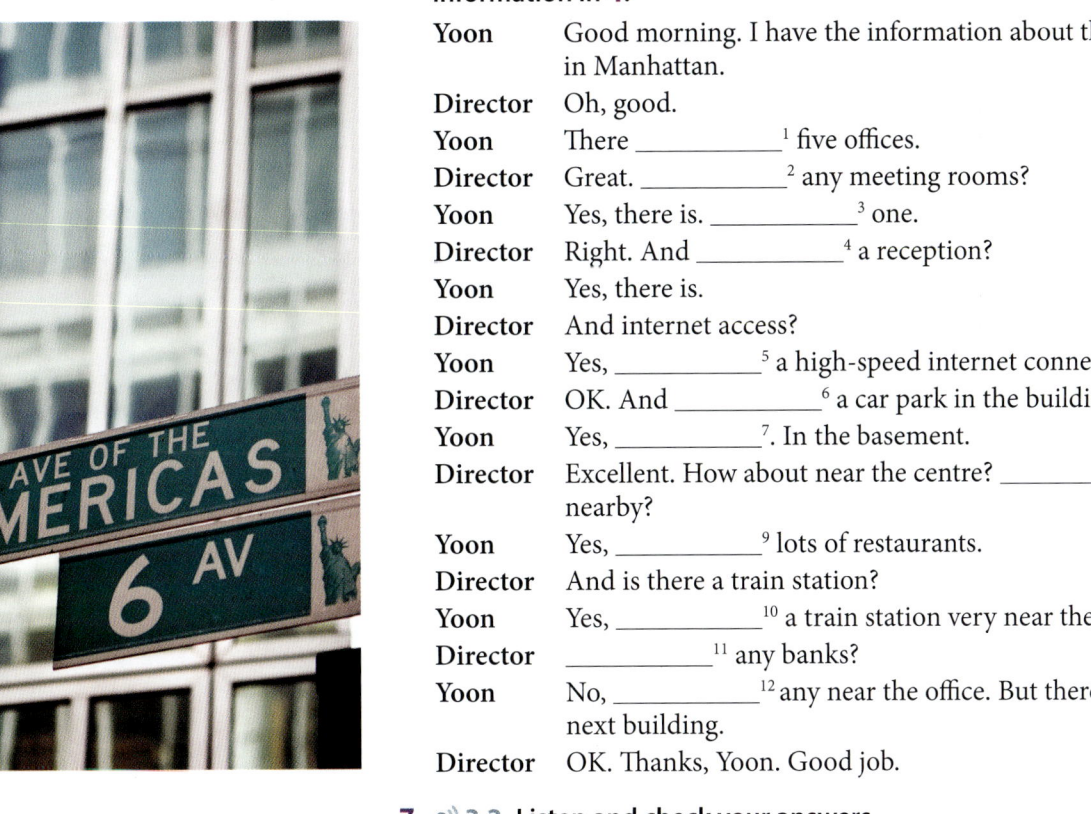

Yoon	Good morning. I have the information about the MyOffice centre in Manhattan.
Director	Oh, good.
Yoon	There _____ [1] five offices.
Director	Great. _____ [2] any meeting rooms?
Yoon	Yes, there is. _____ [3] one.
Director	Right. And _____ [4] a reception?
Yoon	Yes, there is.
Director	And internet access?
Yoon	Yes, _____ [5] a high-speed internet connection.
Director	OK. And _____ [6] a car park in the building?
Yoon	Yes, _____ [7]. In the basement.
Director	Excellent. How about near the centre? _____ [8] any restaurants nearby?
Yoon	Yes, _____ [9] lots of restaurants.
Director	And is there a train station?
Yoon	Yes, _____ [10] a train station very near the centre.
Director	_____ [11] any banks?
Yoon	No, _____ [12] any near the office. But there's an ATM in the next building.
Director	OK. Thanks, Yoon. Good job.

7 ◉⑴ **3.2** Listen and check your answers.

8 Work in pairs. Practise the conversation in **6**.

TASK

9 Work in pairs. Ask and answer about your workplace. Use these words.

reception   meeting rooms   restaurant   coffee shop   banks   car park   offices

Example **A** Is there a reception in your company / school / business centre?
B Yes, there is. / No, there isn't.

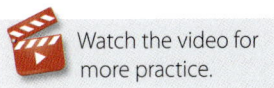
Watch the video for more practice.

10 Report back to a different partner.

Example In (Tariq's) company there _____ a reception. There _____ three meeting rooms …

Vocabulary My workstation

1 ●) **3.3** Look at the picture. Listen and repeat.

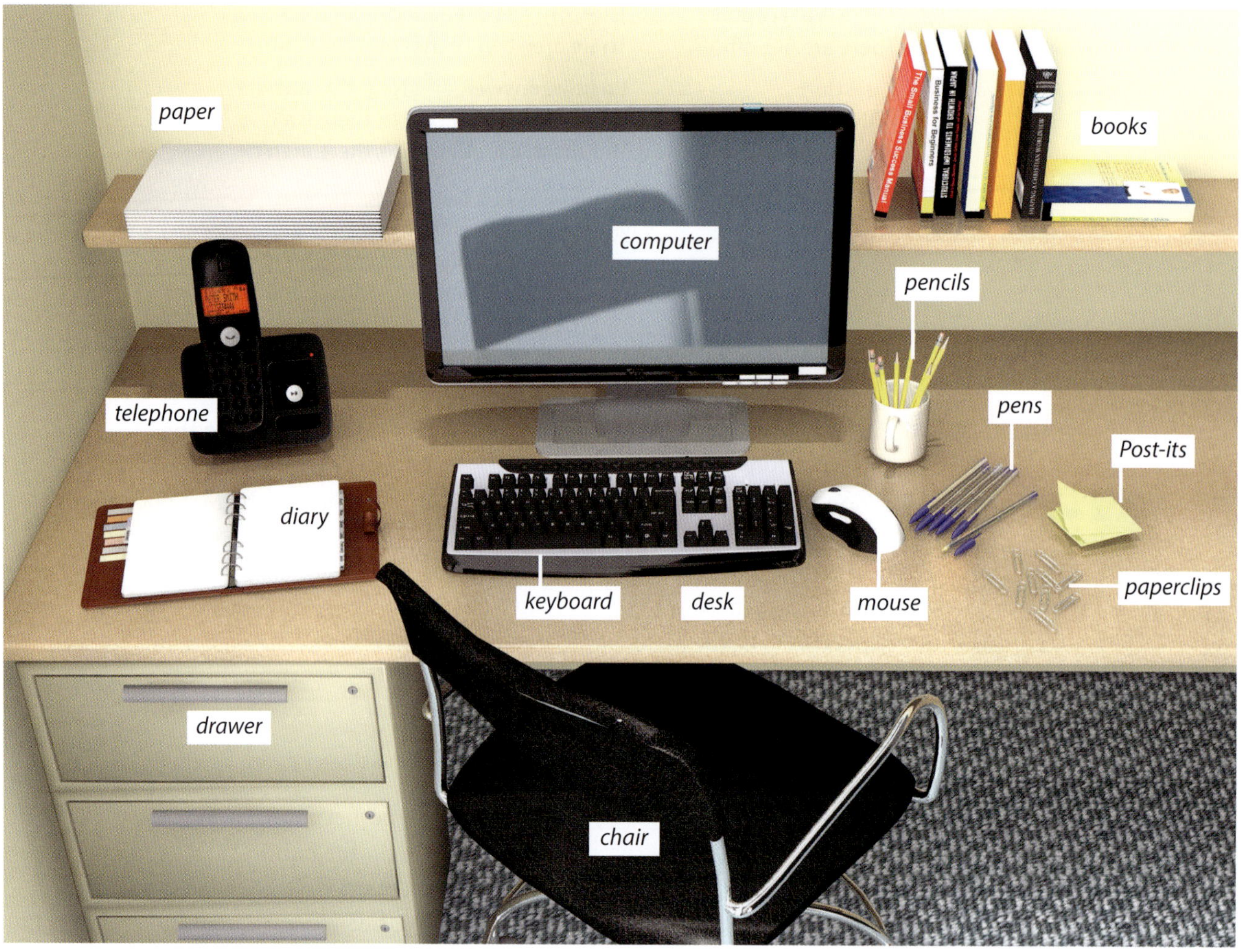

paper

books

computer

pencils

telephone

pens

Post-its

diary

paperclips

keyboard   desk   mouse

drawer

chair

2 ●) **3.4** Barbara talks about her workstation. Listen and tick ✓ the things you hear.

	Barbara	You	Your partner
Post-its			
a keyboard			
a mouse			
a telephone			
paper			
a diary			
pencils			
pens			
a computer			
paperclips			
a drawer			

3 Complete the table for your workstation or desk.

4 Work in pairs. Talk about your workstations or desks. Complete the table for your partner.

Example   Is there a computer on your workstation?

Work skills Emails 1

1 Read the four emails. Match the pairs.

A

From:	Sara Gonzales
To:	alhussein@grif.com
Cc:	readr@rothen.co.uk
Subject:	Details of visit
Sent:	12.07.2013
Attachment:	

Dear Mr Hussein
Please find attached the agenda for the meeting with
Ms Read. Is 11.00 a.m. convenient for you?
With best wishes,
Sara Gonzales
Personal Assistant to Ms Read

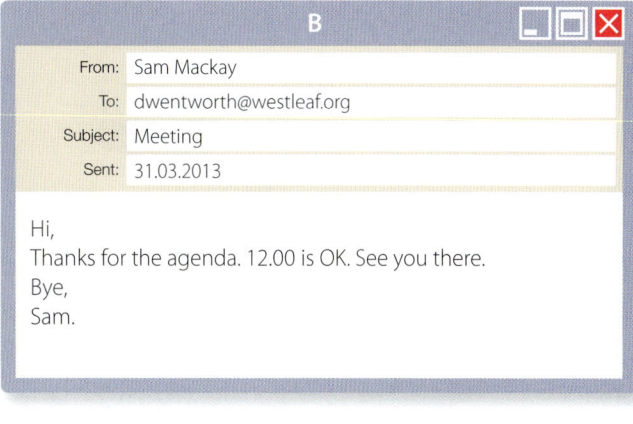

B

From:	Sam Mackay
To:	dwentworth@westleaf.org
Subject:	Meeting
Sent:	31.03.2013

Hi,
Thanks for the agenda. 12.00 is OK. See you there.
Bye,
Sam.

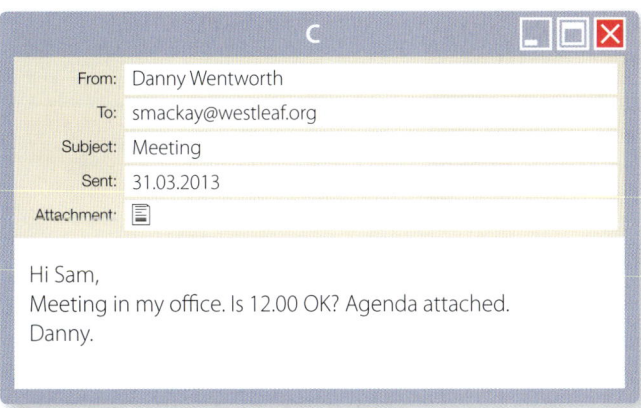

C

From:	Danny Wentworth
To:	smackay@westleaf.org
Subject:	Meeting
Sent:	31.03.2013
Attachment:	

Hi Sam,
Meeting in my office. Is 12.00 OK? Agenda attached.
Danny.

D

From:	Mohammad Hussein
To:	gonzaless@rothen.co.uk
Cc:	readr@rothen.co.uk
Subject:	Details of visit
Sent:	13.07.2013

Dear Ms Gonzales,
Thank you for your email. 11.00 is fine. I look forward to
meeting you and Ms Read.
Best regards,
Mohammad Hussein
Regional Director

2 Read the emails again. Answer the questions.

1 Are Sam and Danny in the same company? _____
2 Are Mr Hussein and Ms Read in the same company? _____
3 Are Sam and Danny colleagues? _____
4 Are Mr Hussein and Ms Read colleagues? _____

3 Complete the table with these words.

Ms Gonzales   Bye   Mr Hussein   Hi   Agenda attached.   Is 11.00 a.m. convenient for you?

Emails	Opening	Names	Main message	Question	Closing
B and C	_____ 1	Sam Danny	_____ 2	Is 12.00 OK?	_____ 3
A and D	Dear	_____ 4 _____ 5	Please find attached the agenda for the meeting with Ms Read.	_____ 6	Best regards With best wishes

Functions Offering and accepting food and drinks

INTRODUCTION **1** 3.5 **Listen and repeat.**

mineral water
apple juice
tea
espresso
coffee
still natural
Mineral Water
APPLE
JUICE
chocolate
cake
fruit
yoghurt
Cheese
Tuna
Fresh
cheese
sandwich
Orange
Juice
orange
juice
tuna
sandwich
Plain
YOGHURT
Fruit
YOGHURT
plain
yoghurt

2 3.6 **Nick Clark takes some visitors to the company canteen. Listen. What do the visitors eat and drink?**

Mona ______________________________

Kim ______________________________

Note ______________________________

3 3.6 **Listen again. Complete the conversations.**

Nick ________[1] you like something to drink, Mona?
Mona Yes, please.
Nick ________[2] would you like?
Mona Is there any ____________[3]?
Nick Yes, there is.
Mona OK. An ____________[4], please.
Nick Right.
Mona Thank you.
…
Nick ________[5] you like something to eat, Kim?
Kim Yes, please.
Nick ________[6] would you like?
Kim ________[7] like a ____________[8], please.
Nick OK. Cheese or tuna?
Kim Cheese, please.
…
Nick ________[9] would you like, Note?
Note I'd ________[10] some apple juice, please.
Nick I'm sorry. There isn't any apple juice. There's orange.
Note OK. An ________[11] juice, ________[12].
Nick Fine. Would you like something to eat?
Note No, thanks.

Focus

Complete the table with these phrases.

I'd like a coffee, please.
Would you like something to drink/eat?
No, thanks.
An orange juice, please.

Offering	Replying
	Yes, please.
What would you like?	

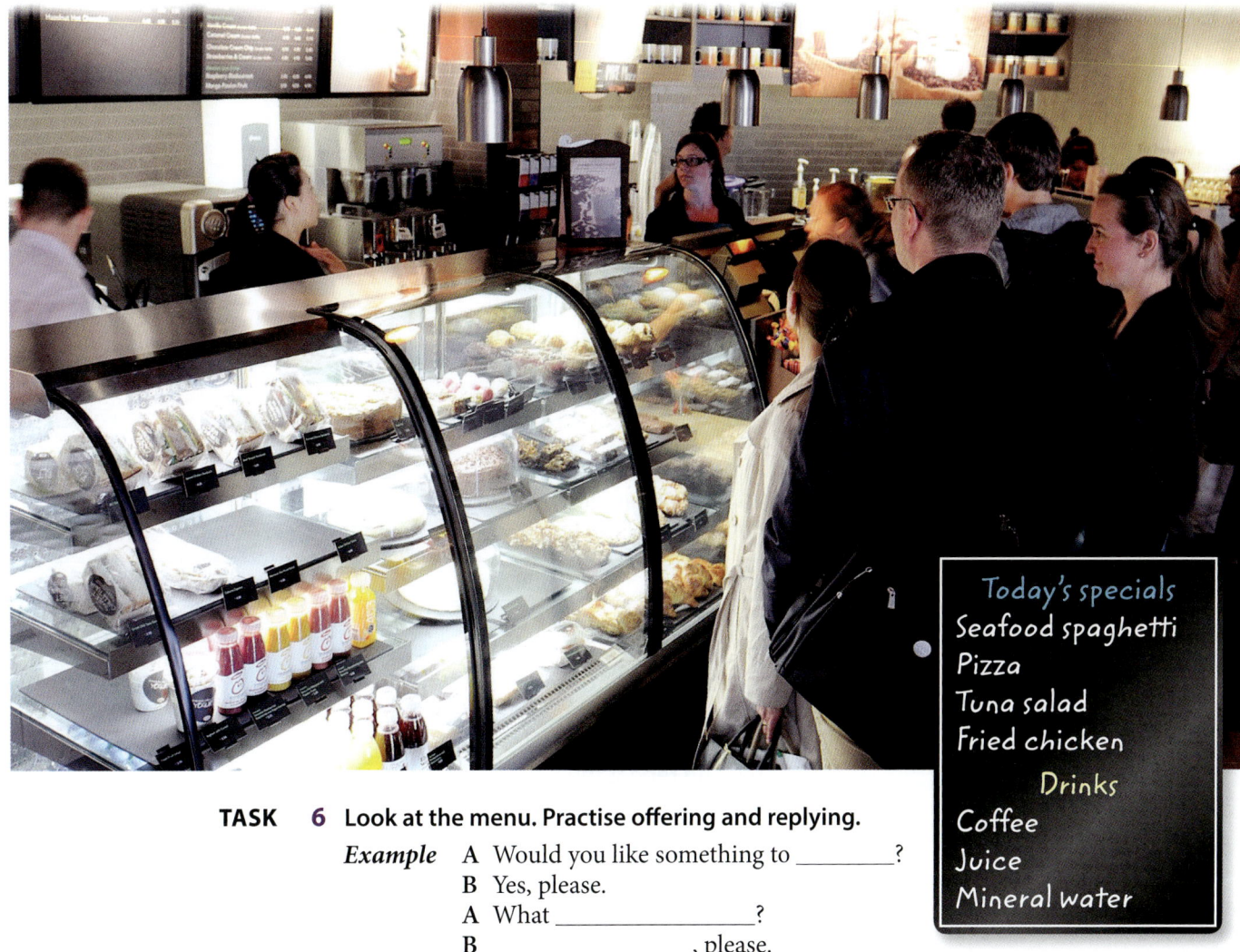

For more details and practice, go to the Review section on page 35.

PRACTICE   **4**   Work in pairs. Practise the conversations in **3**.

5   ◄) **3.7**   Listen and repeat.

Would you like something to eat?
Yes, please.
What would you like?
I'd like a yoghurt, please.
Plain or fruit?
Fruit, please.

Today's specials
Seafood spaghetti
Pizza
Tuna salad
Fried chicken
Drinks
Coffee
Juice
Mineral water

TASK   **6**   Look at the menu. Practise offering and replying.

Example   A   Would you like something to _____?
           B   Yes, please.
           A   What _____?
           B   _____, please.
           A   Right / OK / Fine.

Review

Grammar *there is, there are*

Form

	Positive	Negative
Singular	There is a restaurant.	There isn't a restaurant.
Plural	There are two coffee shops.	There aren't any offices.

Question	Positive answer	Negative answer
Is there a gym?	Yes, there is.	No, there isn't.
Are there any banks?	Yes, there are.	No, there aren't.

We usually use short forms of the positive sentences when we speak.
Examples There's a restaurant.
There're two coffee shops.

We use the word *any* in plural questions and negatives.
Examples Are there any coffee shops?
There aren't any coffee shops.

We do not use the word *any* in short negative answers.
Example A Are there any banks? B No, there aren't.

●)) 3.8 **Listen and repeat the sentences.**

Use

We use *there is* + *a* or *an* with one thing.
Example There is a restaurant.

We use *there are* with two or more things.
Example There are two coffee shops.

Plural nouns

Form

To make a singular noun plural, we usually add an -*s*.
The -*s* at the end of a plural noun can be pronounced /s/, /z/, or /ɪz/.

Singular noun	Plural noun	Pronunciation
restaurant	restaurants	/s/
room	rooms	/z/
office	offices	/ɪz/

●)) 3.9 **Listen and repeat the plural nouns.**

PRACTICE

1 ◾)) **3.10 Listen and put these plural nouns in the correct group.**

rooms   toilets   offices   banks   car parks   centres   managers   bosses   conferences

/s/	/z/	/ɪz/

2 Correct the mistakes.

1   A   There is a restaurant? _____
    B   Yes, there is. _____
2   There is eight meeting rooms. _____
3   There isn't any offices at the moment. _____
4   There are a conference room. _____
5   There aren't a car park. _____
6   A   Is there any banks? _____
    B   No, there are. _____

3 Complete the conversation.

A   Good afternoon. MyOffice. How can I help you?

B   Good afternoon. My name's Ashley Martin. I'm the office manager from Print Express. We want to rent offices in Miami.

A   No problem. _____[1] a big centre with twelve floors in the centre of Miami.

B   We want office space for twenty staff.

A   OK. _____[2] offices available on the first floor.

B   Is there a meeting room?

A   Yes, _____[3] three rooms.

B   _____[4] a kitchen?

A   No, there isn't. But there is a coffee lounge with a drinks machine.

B   OK. And a reception area?

A   Yes, _____[5] a reception desk and waiting area near the lift.

B   That sounds good. _____[6] any shops or restaurants near the centre?

A   Yes, there are lots of places to eat and _____[7] a shopping mall on Lincoln Road.

B   _____[8] any train stations nearby?

A   No. Most people come to work by car.

4 Answer the questions about the conversation in 3.

1   Is there a meeting room? _____
2   Is there a kitchen? _____
3   Is there a drinks machine? _____
4   Are there any shops? _____
5   Are there any stations nearby? _____

Vocabulary My workstation

Label the pictures.

1 _____

2 _____

3 _____

4 _____

5 _____

6 _____

7 _____

8 _____

9 _____

10 _____

Work skills Emails 1

Write the start and ending of the emails.

1

To: Daniel_Shaw@nodoc.com
From: b.gorrin@tmd.com
Subject: Go Magazine article

_____
Could you call me at my office today to talk about the Go Magazine article?
My number is 01345 912367.

_____
Ms Gorrin
Head of Communications

2

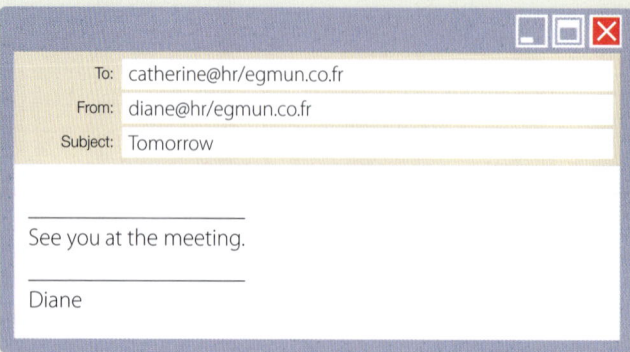

To: catherine@hr/egmun.co.fr
From: diane@hr/egmun.co.fr
Subject: Tomorrow

_____
See you at the meeting.

_____
Diane

Functions Offering and accepting food and drinks

We use *Would …?* or *What would …?* to offer people something to drink or eat.
We reply to *Would you …?* with *Yes, please* or *No, thanks*.
We reply to *What would you like …?* with *I'd like …, please* or *A …, please*.

Example   A   Would you like a drink?
             B   Yes, please.
             A   What would you like?
             B   I'd like an orange juice, please.

PRACTICE   **1**   ◗)) **3.11**   **Listen and tick ✓ the items you hear.**

a ☐   b ☐   c ☐   d ☐   e ☐   f ☐

2   Complete the conversation.

Bob   _____¹ a drink, Liz?
Liz   Yes, please.
Bob   _____²? Coffee, tea, water?
Liz   _____³ water, please.
Bob   _____⁴ something to eat?
Liz   Um … yes, _____⁵ a cake, please.

3   Choose the best answer to the questions.

1   Would you like a drink?
    a Yes, please.   b I'd like a sandwich, please.
2   Can I get you something?
    a No, thanks.   b Milk and sugar, please.
3   What would you like?
    a I'd like a cola, please.   b Yes, please.
4   Ham or cheese?
    a I'd like a sandwich, please.   b Cheese, please.

4 Ready to go

Grammar *have got, has got*

1 ◗)) **4.1 Listen and repeat.**

credit cards ☐

a mobile phone ☐

a passport ☐

plane tickets ☐

money ☐

documents ☐

a gift ☐

business cards ☐

a laptop ☐

2 ◗)) **4.2 Ella MacFarlane and Becky Roberts are on a business trip. Listen to Ella talk to her PA (personal assistant), Mike Jones. Tick ✓ the items Ella and Becky have got in 1.**

3 ◗)) **4.2 Listen again. Complete the conversation with these words.**

Yes   got   Has   they've   No   Have   hasn't   haven't

Mike	Hi, Ella. How are you?
Ella	Fine thanks, Mike.
Mike	_____¹ you got everything?
Ella	Yes, I have. Don't worry! I've _____² my passport, laptop, credit cards, and money.
Mike	_____³ Becky got the plane tickets?
Ella	No, she _____⁴. She's got the code on her mobile phone.
Mike	OK. Have you got the business cards?
Ella	Becky, have we got the business cards? … _____⁵, we have.
Mike	Great. Have you got the documents?
Ella	No, I _____⁶. Becky, have you got the documents? … Yes, she has.
Mike	OK, have a good trip.
Ella	Thanks.
Mike	Oh, and have you got a gift for Mr Yamamoto?
Ella	_____⁷, we haven't! But _____⁸ got British souvenirs in the shops at the airport …

Focus

Read the examples.

Long form	**Short form**	**Negative**
I **have got** a laptop.	I**'ve got** a laptop.	I **haven't got** a laptop.
He **has got** a passport.	He**'s got** a passport.	He **hasn't got** a passport.

Questions	**Positive answer**	**Negative answer**
Have you **got** a credit card?	Yes, I **have**.	No, I **haven't**.
Has she **got** the documents?	Yes, she **has**.	No, she **hasn't**.

Complete the rules.

To make positive sentences, we use *I/you/we/they* + _____ + *got*, or *he/she/it* + _____ + *got*.

To make questions, we use _____ + *I/you/we/they* + *got*, or *Has* + _____ + *got*.

To make negative sentences and answers, we use _____ + *n't got*, or _____ + *n't got*.

▶▶ For more details and practice, go to the Review section on pages 42 and 43.

PRACTICE

4 Write the questions.

1 (Ella / her passport)? *Has Ella got her passport?* _____
2 (Ella / her laptop)? _____
3 (Becky / the plane tickets)? _____
4 (they / the business cards)? _____
5 (Ella / the documents)? _____
6 (they / a gift)? _____
7 (Ella / a mobile phone)? _____

5 Work in pairs. Ask and answer the questions in 4.

Example   A Has Ella got her passport?
B Yes, she's got her passport. / Yes, she has.

6 Read the article in *High Flyer* magazine.

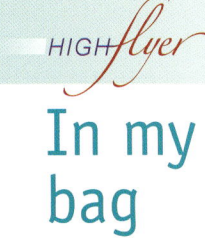

In my bag

Todd Blakey

What have I got in my bag? Well, I've got a mobile phone. It's got the phone numbers and email addresses of friends and work colleagues. And I've got a laptop. I've got business cards. I've got a book. I haven't got any money or credit cards. And I've got my passport, of course!

Tanja Larsson

I haven't got much in my bag. I haven't got a laptop or any documents. I've got my pen and a notebook. I've got a mobile phone. I haven't got any business cards. I have got my money, credit cards, and my passport. Oh, and I've got gifts for my colleagues.

7 Work in pairs. You are Todd and Tanja. Ask questions.

Example   A Todd, have you got a mobile phone?
B Yes, I have.

TASK

8 Work in pairs.

Student A You are going on holiday. Choose six things to put in your bag.
Student B You are going on a business trip. Choose six things to put in your bag.

Ask and answer questions about the things in your bags.

Example   A Have you got a passport?
B Yes, I have. / No, I haven't.

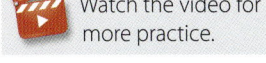
Watch the video for more practice.

Vocabulary Days, months, and dates

1 ◗)) **4.3** **Listen and complete the days of the week.**

M___day   T___day   Wednesday   Th___day   F___day   Saturday   S___day

2 ◗)) **4.3** **Listen again and repeat.**

3 **Complete the sentences.**

Today is _____. Tomorrow is _____.
My English class is on _____.
The weekend is _____ and _____.

4 ◗)) **4.4** **Listen and write the months in the calendar.**

February   July   April   October   May   December

January

S	M	T	W	T	F	S
					1	2
3	4	5	6	7	8	9
10	11	12	13	14	15	16
17	18	19	20	21	22	23
24	25	26	27	28	29	30
31						

_____ 1

S	M	T	W	T	F	S
1	2	3	4	5	6	
7	8	9	10	11	12	13
14	15	16	17	18	19	20
21	22	23	24	25	26	27
28						

March

S	M	T	W	T	F	S
1	2	3	4	5	6	
7	8	9	10	11	12	13
14	15	16	17	18	19	20
21	22	23	24	25	26	27
28	29	30	31			

_____ 2

S	M	T	W	T	F	S
				1	2	3
4	5	6	7	8	9	10
11	12	13	14	15	16	17
18	19	20	21	22	23	24
25	26	27	28	29	30	

_____ 3

S	M	T	W	T	F	S
1						
2	3	4	5	6	7	8
9	10	11	12	13	14	15
16	17	18	19	20	21	22
23	24	25	26	27	28	29
30	31					

June

S	M	T	W	T	F	S
		1	2	3	4	5
6	7	8	9	10	11	12
13	14	15	16	17	18	19
20	21	22	23	24	25	26
27	28	29	30			

_____ 4

S	M	T	W	T	F	S
				1	2	3
4	5	6	7	8	9	10
11	12	13	14	15	16	17
18	19	20	21	22	23	24
25	26	27	28	29	30	31

August

S	M	T	W	T	F	S
1	2	3	4	5	6	7
8	9	10	11	12	13	14
15	16	17	18	19	20	21
22	23	24	25	26	27	28
29	30	31				

September

S	M	T	W	T	F	S
			1	2	3	4
5	6	7	8	9	10	11
12	13	14	15	16	17	18
19	20	21	22	23	24	25
26	27	28	29	30		

_____ 5

S	M	T	W	T	F	S
					1	2
3	4	5	6	7	8	9
10	11	12	13	14	15	16
17	18	19	20	21	22	23
24	25	26	27	28	29	30
31						

November

S	M	T	W	T	F	S
	1	2	3	4	5	6
7	8	9	10	11	12	13
14	15	16	17	18	19	20
21	22	23	24	25	26	27
28	29	30				

_____ 6

S	M	T	W	T	F	S
			1	2	3	4
5	6	7	8	9	10	11
12	13	14	15	16	17	18
19	20	21	22	23	24	25
26	27	28	29	30	31	

5 **Complete the sentences with a month.**

This month is _____.
My birthday is in _____.
My summer holiday is in _____.
The business/school year starts in _____.

6 ◗)) **4.5** **Listen and repeat.**

first   second   third   fourth   fifth   sixth   seventh   eighth   ninth
tenth   eleventh   twelfth   thirteenth   fourteenth   fifteenth   sixteenth
seventeenth   eighteenth   nineteenth   twentieth   twenty-first   thirtieth

7 **Look at the calendar. What days are these dates?**

1   6th March   *Saturday, the sixth of March / Saturday, March the sixth*
2   8th February   _____
3   15th June   _____
4   26th August   _____
5   2nd April   _____
6   11th September   _____
7   16th May   _____
8   3rd November   _____

8 ◗)) **4.6** **Listen and circle the dates you hear on the calendar.**

9 **Complete the sentences.**

The date today is _____.
My birthday is _____.
This year, the _____ festival is on _____.

10 ◗)) **4.7** **Listen and repeat the years.**

2014   1914   1814   2001   1901   1801

Work skills Telephoning 1

1 ●)) **4.8 Listen. Complete the telephone conversation with these words.**

calling   Could   speaking   How   It's

Receiver	Good **morning**, KLF Limited. _____¹ can I help you?
Caller	Good morning. _____² I speak to **Lisa Chang**, please?
Receiver	Certainly. Can I take your name, please?
Caller	Yes. _____³ **Juan Carlos Rodriguez**.
Receiver	Thank you, **Mr Rodriguez**. Please hold the line.
Caller	Thank you.
Lisa Chang	**Lisa Chang** _____⁴.
Caller	Hi, **Lisa**. It's **Juan Carlos** from **Novotec**.
Lisa Chang	Oh, hi **Juan**. How are you?
Caller	Fine, thanks. I'm _____⁵ about our meeting on **Monday** …

2 **Are the sentences true or false?**

		True	False
1	Juan Carlos Rodriguez works for KLF Limited.	☐	☐
2	He wants to speak to Lisa Chang.	☐	☐
3	Lisa Chang works for KLF Limited.	☐	☐
4	Lisa Chang knows Juan Carlos.	☐	☐
5	Juan Carlos is calling about a problem.	☐	☐

3 **Work in threes. Practise the telephone conversation in 1.**

4 **Practise the conversation again. Change the highlighted words.**

afternoon   Mari Gomez   Franz Müller   SkyNet   Friday

5 **Work in threes. Role-play this telephone conversation.**

Student A	You are the receiver. You work for Data Systems.
Student B	You are the caller. Use your name. You work for PetroLine. Ask to speak to Antony Roddick. You are calling about a meeting on Thursday.
Student C	You work for Data Systems. Your name is Antony Roddick. You know the caller.

Functions Making an arrangement

1 ●)) **4.9** Look at Karla's schedule. Listen to Jacques and Karla making an arrangement. Complete Karla's calendar entry.

Schedule

Monday	Tuesday	Wednesday	Thursday	Friday	Saturday	Sunday
30 June	1 July	2 July	3 July	4 July	5 July	6 July
Morning		*Meeting 10–12*				
Afternoon *Meeting 2–5*	*Presentation 2–5*		*Business trip*	*Visiting a company 2–5*	*Weekend*	

Calendar entry

Activity	*Meeting*	1
Day		2
Date		3
Time		4
Place		5

2 Order the conversation.

Jacques	Hello, is that Karla? It's Jacques Brennard here.	___
Jacques	Thanks! Bye.	___
Jacques	Are you free on Wednesday morning for a meeting?	___
Jacques	Yes, the afternoon is OK. How about two o'clock?	___
Karla	OK. See you then.	___
Karla	Hi, Jacques. How can I help you?	___
Karla	Let me check … I'm sorry, I'm busy on Wednesday morning. How about in the afternoon?	___
Jacques	Great. So my office on Wednesday at two o'clock.	___
Karla	Yes, two o'clock is fine with me.	___

3 ●)) **4.9** Listen again and check. Practise the conversation in pairs.

Focus

Complete the rules with these phrases.

I'm sorry, I'm busy.   Are you free …?   How about …?   … is fine with me.   … is OK.

We use _____ or _____ to ask about the day and time.

We use _____ or _____ when we are free.

We use _____ when we are not free.

Match the prepositions with the days/times.

in   six o'clock, seven thirty
on   the morning, the afternoon
at   Monday, Tuesday afternoon

● For more details and practice, go to the Review section on page 45.

4 Complete the sentences with words from the Focus section.

1 Are you free _____ Friday?
2 There's a sales meeting _____ the morning.
3 I'm sorry. I'm busy _____ Thursday morning.
4 Let's meet _____ 1.15 in my office.
5 The meeting is _____ 4.30 _____ Monday afternoon.
6 Tuesday afternoon is _____ _____ me.
7 I'm busy in the morning but the afternoon is _____.
8 How _____ 5.00?
9 My business trip is _____ Thursday.
10 The presentation finishes _____ five o'clock.

5 Ask and answer questions about Karla's schedule in 1.

Example **A** Is Karla free on Monday afternoon?
              B No, she's busy. She's in a meeting.
              A How about Tuesday morning?
              B Yes, she's free in the morning.

TASK **6 Work in pairs. Make an arrangement.**

A	B
Are you free on [day] [morning/afternoon] for a meeting?	
	I'm sorry, I'm busy. How about in the [morning/afternoon]?
Yes, the [morning/afternoon] is OK. How about [time] o'clock?	
	Yes, [time] o'clock is fine with me.
Great. So my office on [day] at [time].	
	OK. See you then.
Thanks! Bye.	

Review

Grammar *have got, has got*

Form

Positive (long form)	Positive (short form)	Negative (short form)
I have got a laptop.	I've got a laptop.	I haven't got a laptop.
He has got a credit card.	He's got a credit card.	He hasn't got a credit card.
She has got a business card.	She's got a business card.	She hasn't got a business card.
It has got a shop.	It's got a shop.	It hasn't got a shop.
We have got the documents.	We've got the documents.	We haven't got the documents.
They have got a gift.	They've got a gift.	They haven't got a gift.

Question	Positive answer	Negative answer
Have you got a laptop?	Yes, I have.	No, I haven't.
Has he got a credit card?	Yes, he has.	No, he hasn't.
Has she got a business card?	Yes, she has.	No, she hasn't.
Has it got a shop?	Yes, it has.	No, it hasn't.
Have you got the documents?	Yes, we have.	No, we haven't.
Have we got the plane tickets?	Yes, we have.	No, we haven't.
Have they got a gift?	Yes, they have.	No, they haven't.

We usually use short forms of the positive sentences when we speak.
Example   He's got a laptop.

We use *any* in plural questions and negatives.
Examples Have you got any business cards?
            He hasn't got any credit cards.

American English and British English
We use both *have* and *have got* in British English.
Examples I have my mobile phone.
            I've got my mobile phone.

We only use *have* in American English.

●)) 4.10 **Listen and repeat the short forms.**

Use

We use *have got* to ask and answer about the items we carry.
Examples A Have you got a pen in your bag?   B No, I haven't.
            They've got the plane tickets.

We use *have got* to talk about possessions.
Examples I've got a mobile phone.
            She's got a car.

We use *have got* to talk about relationships with other people.
Examples I've got two children.
            We've got a new boss.

PRACTICE

1 Complete the conversation.

James	How's your new business?
Youssef/Anna	It's great.
James	Youssef, have you got an office?
Youssef	Yes, we _____ [1].
James	And Anna, have you got _____ [2] business cards?
Anna	No, I _____ [3].
James	Have you got a computer?
Anna	Yes, we'_____ [4] got a new computer. And Youssef'_____ [5] got an iPad.
James	Have you both _____ [6] mobile phones?
Youssef	Yes, we _____ [7].
James	Have you got _____ [8] customers?
Youssef	We've got three customers at the moment.

2 Correct the sentences about Anna and Youssef.

	Anna	Youssef
chairs and desks	✓	✓
coffee cups	✓	✓
desk light	✗	✗
printer	✓	✓
plane tickets	✗	✓

1 They haven't got any chairs and desks. *They have got some chairs and desks.*

2 Youssef hasn't got a coffee cup. _____

3 They have got two desk lights. _____

4 Anna hasn't got a printer. _____

5 They have got two plane tickets. _____

3 Complete the questions. Use *have* or *has*.

1 *Have* you got a job?   *b*

2 _____ she got an office?   ___

3 _____ he got a company?   ___

4 _____ they got the tickets?   ___

5 _____ it got a meeting room?   ___

6 _____ you got a meeting today?   ___

4 Match the answers a–f with the questions in 3.

a No, they haven't.

b Yes, I have.

c Yes, it has.

d Yes, he has.

e No, she hasn't.

f Yes, we have.

Vocabulary Days, months, and dates

1 Look at the calendar. Write the days.

1 _Friday_ 1st April
2 _____ 13th April
3 _____ 25th April
4 _____ 2nd April
5 _____ 28th April
6 _____ 17th April
7 _____ 19th April

Mon	Tue	Wed	Thu	Fri	Sat	Sun
28	29	30	31	1	2	3
④	5	6	7	8	9	10
11	⑫	13	14	15	16	17
18	19	20	㉑	22	23	24
25	26	27	28	29	30	1

2 Write the circled dates from the calendar.

_____

_____

_____

3 ◉)) 4.11 Listen and write the dates.

1 Meeting   _____
2 Conference _____

4 ◉)) 4.12 Listen and write the months in the correct group.

o	oO	Oo	Oooo	oOo
	July		January	

5 ◉)) 4.13 Listen and write the years.

1 _____
2 _____
3 _____
4 _____
5 _____
6 _____

Work skills Telephoning 1

1 Complete the telephone conversation.

Receiver Good morning, Technos. How can I _____[1] you?
Caller   Hello. Could I _____[2] Mark Cooke, _____[3]?
Receiver Certainly. Can I _____[4] your name?
Caller   Yes. _____[5] Mohamed Hanif.
Receiver Thank you, Mr Hanif. Please _____[6] the line.
Caller   Thank you.
Mark   Mark Cooke _____[7].
Caller   Hi, Mark. It's Mohamed _____[8] Novotec.
Mark   Oh, hi. _____[9] are you?
Caller   Fine, thanks. I'm calling _____[10] our meeting on Monday …

2 ◉)) 4.14 Listen and check your answers.

Functions Making an arrangement

We use *Are you free … ?* or *How about …?* to ask about the day and time.
Example   Are you free on Tuesday morning for a meeting?

We use *… is fine with me* or *… is OK* when you are free.
Example   Wednesday afternoon is fine with me.

We use *I'm sorry, I'm busy …* when you are not free.
Example   I'm sorry, I'm busy on Friday afternoon.

We use *in* for the parts of the days and months.
in   the morning, the afternoon, the evening
     January, April, October

We use *on* for days and dates.
on   Monday, Saturday
     Wednesday afternoon, Sunday morning
     15th June, 1st December

We use *at* for time.
at   five thirty, 11.15

PRACTICE   **1 Complete the table with these words.**

twelve p.m.   Saturday   1st March   September   ~~the morning~~   6.00 p.m.
Wednesday morning lunchtime   December   the afternoon Monday   Friday evening

in	on	at
the morning		

2 Complete the conversation with these words.

OK   How about (2)   are you free   Thursday   I'm busy   Let me check

Katrina   Hi, Lucy. This is Katrina.
Lucy   Hello, Katrina.
Katrina   Lucy, _____[1] on Friday?
Lucy   _____[2]. No, I'm sorry, _____[3] on Friday. _____[4] Thursday?
Katrina   Yes, Thursday is _____[5].
Lucy   In the morning?
Katrina   Yes. _____[6] 9.00?
Lucy   9.00 is fine with me.
Katrina   Great! Let's meet in the coffee shop.
Lucy   OK. So _____[7] at 9.00 in the coffee shop.
Katrina   Thanks, Lucy. Bye.

3 ◗)) 4.15 Listen and check your answers.

5 Trains & boats & planes

Grammar *he/she/it + verb; Do ...? and Does...?; always, sometimes, never*

INTRODUCTION **1** 5.1 **Listen and read the interviews.**

HIGH*flyer*

Freelancer

Matt Tate lives in Vancouver. He doesn't go to work by train or by car. He walks to the coffee shop near his house.

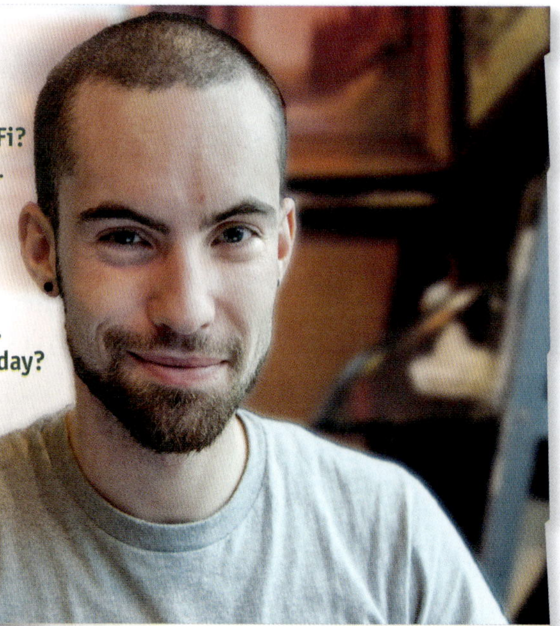

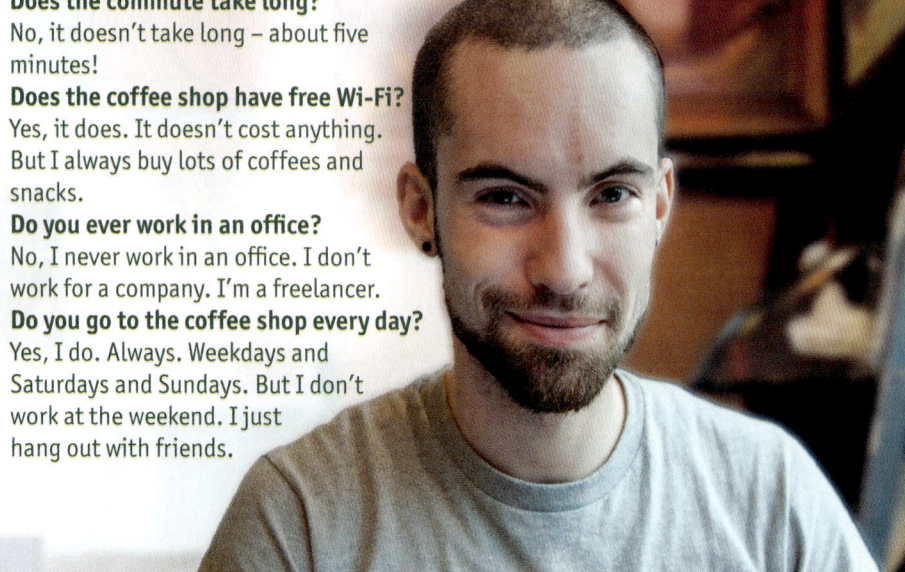

Does the commute take long?
No, it doesn't take long – about five minutes!
Does the coffee shop have free Wi-Fi?
Yes, it does. It doesn't cost anything. But I always buy lots of coffees and snacks.
Do you ever work in an office?
No, I never work in an office. I don't work for a company. I'm a freelancer.
Do you go to the coffee shop every day?
Yes, I do. Always. Weekdays and Saturdays and Sundays. But I don't work at the weekend. I just hang out with friends.

Company worker

Lisa Romero works for an international company in Madrid, Spain. She goes to work by train.

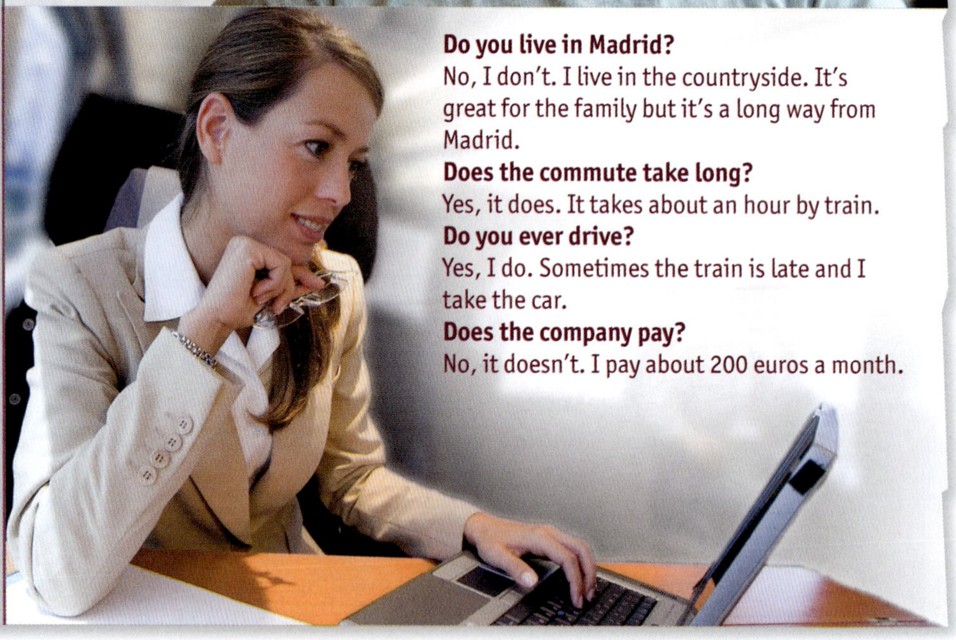

Do you live in Madrid?
No, I don't. I live in the countryside. It's great for the family but it's a long way from Madrid.
Does the commute take long?
Yes, it does. It takes about an hour by train.
Do you ever drive?
Yes, I do. Sometimes the train is late and I take the car.
Does the company pay?
No, it doesn't. I pay about 200 euros a month.

2 **Are the sentences true or false?**

		True	False
1	Matt commutes to work.	☐	☐
2	He works in an office.	☐	☐
3	He doesn't work for a company.	☐	☐
4	He goes to the coffee shop every day.	☐	☐
5	He doesn't work at the weekend.	☐	☐
6	Lisa lives in Madrid.	☐	☐
7	She commutes by train.	☐	☐
8	She never drives to work.	☐	☐

Focus

he/she/it + verb

Positive	Negative
He **walks** to the coffee shop.	He **doesn't commute** to work.

Do ...?* and *Does ...?

Question	Positive answer	Negative answer
Do you ever **drive**?	Yes, I **do**.	No, I **don't**.
Does the commute **take** long?	Yes, it **does**.	No, it **doesn't**.

Complete the rules.

Positive *he/she/it* verbs end in an _____.

To make questions, we use *Do + I/you/we/they* and _____ + *he/she/it*.

To make the negative, we use *don't* and _____.

always, sometimes, never

Find examples of *always*, *sometimes*, and *never* in the interviews. Put them in the correct place.

0% _____   50% _____   100% _____

▶▶ For more details and practice, go to the Review section on pages 52 and 53.

PRACTICE   **3**   **Complete the sentences. Use these verbs and change the endings.**

get up   live   speak   work   eat   go

Egil Andersen comes from Norway but he _____ ¹ in São Paulo in Brazil. He _____ ² for Petrobras, the Brazilian energy company. He sometimes _____ ³ to the main office in Rio de Janeiro.

He commutes three hours a day. He always _____ ⁴ at 6.00 in the morning and gets home at about 9.00 at night.

He loves Brazilian food and always _____ ⁵ lunch at one of the local restaurants. He never eats Norwegian food. He _____ ⁶ English, Norwegian, and Portuguese.

4   •)) **5.2** **Listen and check your answers.**

5   **Put the words in the correct order to make questions.**

1   from does Egil Brazil come?   _____
2   in does he Rio de Janeiro live?   _____
3   in main office is the Petrobras São Paulo? _____
4   get up he at does 6.00?   _____
5   at does 9.30 he get home?   _____
6   does in the office eat lunch he?   _____
7   he Norwegian food eat does?   _____
8   speak he does Portuguese?   _____

6   **Work in pairs. Answer the questions in 5. Use the information in 3.**

7   **Complete the questions with these verbs.**

work   get up   take   speak   drink   eat

1   Do you _____ early?   4   Do you _____ for a big company?
2   Do you _____ coffee?   5   Do you _____ lunch at a restaurant?
3   Do you _____ the train to work? 6   Do you _____ any other languages?

8   **Work in pairs. Ask and answer the questions in 7.**

TASK   **9**   **Tell the class about your partner.**

Example   Ali doesn't get up early. He gets up at 8.30.

Watch the video for more practice.

Vocabulary Getting around

1 **Match the words 1–8 with the pictures a–h.**

1 by car	___	5 by plane	___
2 by train	___	6 on foot	___
3 by bicycle/bike	___	7 by boat/ferry	___
4 by bus	___	8 by taxi	___

2 ◗)) **5.3 Listen. How do these people get to work?**

1 Pedro	*by car*		5 Narumi	_____
2 Lynne	_____		6 Ana	_____
3 Dieter	_____		7 Christian	_____
4 Lee	_____		8 John	_____

3 **Ask and answer about the people in 2.**

Example **A** How does Pedro get to work?
　　　　　B He goes by car.

4 **Work in pairs. Ask and answer questions about getting to work.**

Example **A** How do you get to work?
　　　　　B I go by train. It takes about 40 minutes.

5 **Complete the sentences with these words.**

stand park gate platform pier stop airport

1 The British Airways flight for Tokyo Narita leaves Heathrow _____ at 2.45 from _____ 6.
2 Could you put the bicycle back in the _____ when you return?
3 The ferry to Cheung Chau leaves the Tsim Sha Tsui _____ in five minutes.
4 The car _____ costs €3 per hour.
5 Passengers for the Prince Hotel, get off at the last bus _____ in the city centre.
6 The next train for Firenze leaves _____ 9 at 10.15.

6 ◗)) **5.4 Listen and check your answers.**

7 **Are the sentences true or false?**

	True	False
1 The British Airways flight leaves from gate 5.	☐	☐
2 You leave bicycles on the street when you return them.	☐	☐
3 The ferry to Cheung Chau goes from the Hung Hom pier.	☐	☐
4 Parking costs €3 an hour.	☐	☐
5 The bus for the Prince Hotel goes to the last bus stop in the city centre.	☐	☐
6 The 10.15 train to Firenze leaves from platform 9.	☐	☐

Work skills Telephoning 2

1 ●) **5.5 Listen to the telephone conversation.**

John	Hello. John Davis speaking. Can I help you?
Elena	Could I speak to Rob Gordon, please?
John	I'm sorry. He's in a meeting at the moment. Can I take a message?
Elena	Yes, please. Could you ask him to call me? My name's Elena Moretti. I work in the Milan office.
John	Elena Moretti …
Elena	Yes, that's E-L-E-N-A M-O-R-E-T-T-I.
John	OK. Does he have your number?
Elena	I don't think so. It's 0039.
John	0039.
Elena	8536.
John	8536.
Elena	0001, extension 45.
John	0001, extension 45. Thank you. I'll ask him to call you.
Elena	Thank you. Bye.
John	Bye.

2 Are the sentences true or false?

	True	False
1 Elena Moretti wants to speak to John Davis.	☐	☐
2 Rob Gordon is in a meeting.	☐	☐
3 Elena Moretti leaves a message for Rob Gordon.	☐	☐
4 Her telephone number is 0039 85360011.	☐	☐

3 Complete the email with information from 1.

> Rob,
> Please call _____ ¹ from the _____ ² office. Her number is _____ ³.
> Regards,
> _____ ⁴

4 Match the four parts to make sentences.

	in a	here	
	on	meeting	at the moment.
He's	on a	business trip	today.
She's	out of the	another line	this week.
	on	office	
	not	holiday	

Example He's on holiday this week.

5 Practise these telephone conversations.

1	Receiver	Use your own name.
	Caller	Sanjay Gupta Jaipur office
	Wants to speak to	Françoise Dupré
		Françoise is out of the office.
	Caller's number	011-20000198
		Extension 357

2	Receiver	Use your own name.
	Caller	Nasser Al-Johar Riyadh office
	Wants to speak to	Juan Fernandez
		Juan is on another line.
	Caller's number	966 01 766 4455
		Extension 253

Functions Talking about things you like; making suggestions

INTRODUCTION **1** Read about places to visit in London. Match the places 1–3 with the pictures a–c. Which places do you like?

1 Holland Park

How about a quiet walk on Sunday morning? You can enjoy the beautiful flower gardens and open spaces. It's all free and great for kids.

2 Victoria and Albert Museum

Do you like art, fashion, and beautiful buildings? Then we suggest you try this amazing collection of paintings, photos, furniture, and jewellery.

3 Harvey Nichols

This famous department store has got great fashion floors for men and women, a wonderful food store, and a great restaurant on the top floor.

2 ◗) **5.6** Kenichi Hashimoto from Nissin visits Premier Foods, a customer in London. Lara Flynn talks to him about his free day. Listen and complete the table.

	likes	Lara's suggestions
Kenichi		
Wife		
Daughter		

Focus

Read the examples.

She really **likes** department stores.
I **like** walking.

Complete the rules with *verb -ing* or *noun*.

We use *like* + _____ to talk about things we like.
We use *like* + _____ to talk about activities we like.

Read the examples.

How about going to a park first?
Why don't you go to Harvey Nichols?

Complete the rule.

To make suggestions, we use *How about* + _____ or *Why don't you* + _____.

▶▶ For more details and practice, go to the Review section on page 55.

PRACTICE   **3**   Work in pairs. Practise the conversation. Use *How about …?* or *Why don't you …?*

A Are you free tomorrow?
B Yes, I am.
A Do you like **sightseeing**?
B Yes, I do.
A OK. Why don't you **go to the London Eye**?
B That's a good idea.

1 shopping, go/going to Harrods
2 Italian food, have/having lunch at the Spaghetti House
3 music, go/going to a concert at the Royal Albert Hall
4 walking, visit/visiting Hyde Park
5 art, visit/visiting the National Gallery
6 sightseeing, go/going on the City Sightseeing Bus
7 British food, try/trying some fish and chips
8 theatre, see/seeing a play at the National Theatre
9 films, watch/watching a film in Leicester Square
10 modern buildings, take/taking a tour of the City

TASK   **4**   Work in pairs. A visitor comes to your country. Ask them about the things they like / like doing. Suggest some things they can do or places to visit.

Sightseeing   Eating out   Music, theatre, and films
Culture and art   Shopping

Review

Grammar *he/she/it* + verb; *Do …?* and *Does …?*

Form

To make most verbs in the third person, we add *-s*.
Example   He walks to the coffee shop.

To make the negative, we use *doesn't*.
Example   He doesn't commute to work.
To make a question, we use *Do …?* or *Does …?*

Question	Short answer
Do you sometimes drive?	Yes, I do.
Do you live in Madrid?	No, I don't.
Does the commute take long?	Yes, it does.
Does the company pay?	No, it doesn't.

Third person *-s*: some spelling rules

For verbs that end in *s*, *sh*, *ch*, *x* or *z*, and *o*, we add *-es*.
Examples He watches TV.
        He goes to Zurich every week.

For verbs that end in a consonant + *y*, we change *y* to *ie*, then add *-s*.
Example   study – She studies at the weekend.

For verbs endings in vowel + *y*, add *-s*.
Example   play – He plays tennis for his company team.

Use

We use the third person *-s* when we talk about people with *he* or *she*.
Example   He lives in Dubai.

We also use the third person *-s* to talk about things with *it*.
Example   It costs 50 euros.

We use *do* and *does* to make questions about facts, habits, and the present situation.

•)) 5.7 **Listen. Put these words in the correct group.**

eats   lives   speaks   does   buys   gets

/s/	/z/
works	goes

always, sometimes, never

Form

Always, *sometimes*, and *never* are called adverbs of frequency.
We put adverbs of frequency before most verbs.
We put adverbs of frequency after the verb *be*.

Examples He sometimes goes to work by train.
              She is always busy on Monday mornings.

Always goes between the person and the verb in *do* questions.
Examples **A** Do you always go to work by bus?   **B** No, I don't.
              A Does she always have a meeting on Monday? **B** Yes, she does.

Use

We use adverbs of frequency to say how often or how regularly we do things.
Examples I sometimes meet friends for lunch.
              He always travels by bike.

Never = 0%; sometimes = 50%; always = 100%.

PRACTICE

1 Complete the sentences. Use the verb with the correct ending.

1   work   He *works*____ for a software design company in Chile.
2   live   _____ he _____ in Abu Dhabi?
3   go   He _____ to China once a month for meetings.
4   not have   He _____ _____ a car.
5   study   He _____ Chinese in his free time.
6   work   _____ she _____ in an office?
7   have   She _____ her own business.
8   design   She _____ websites.
9   not speak   She _____ _____ Spanish.
10 travel   She _____ to Italy three or four times a month.

2 Complete the text. Write the correct form of the verbs in brackets.

Ahmed Miftahi _____[1] (use) three languages at work: English, French, and
Arabic. He _____[2] (work) at the head office of a building company in Rabat,
in Morocco. It's an international office and there _____[3] (be) people from
many different countries in the office. They usually _____[4] (speak) together in
English or French. Ahmed usually _____[5] (speak) English with his workmates
in the office, and Arabic when he _____[6] (talk) to his colleagues in the Middle
East. He _____[7] (do not travel) much in his job, but he _____[8]
(enjoy) his work in an international office.

3 Read the example questions and answers. Complete the questions and answers.

Examples Do you live in Salvador? No, I don't.
              Does she work in IT?   No, she doesn't.

1   _____ work for Apple?   No, he _____.
2   _____ have a meeting today? Yes, we _____. It's this afternoon at 3.15.
3   _____ work on Fridays?   No, she _____. Please try again on Monday.
4   _____ leave at 9.20?   Yes, it _____. From platform 9.

4 **Put the words in the correct order to make questions.**

1 you do in an work office? _____
2 speak do English at work you? _____
3 boss does speak your English? _____
4 by do you go to work car? _____
5 have does a website your company? _____
6 go business trips do you on? _____
7 home do get late you? _____

5 **Write the answers to the questions in 4.**

Vocabulary Getting around

1 **Complete the texts using the words under the pictures.**

New York   15 minutes   on foot
Natalie   bank

train   Paris   design   1 hour   Marc

My name is _____¹. I live in _____². I work for an international _____³. I go to work _____⁴. It takes about _____⁵.

I'm _____⁶. I live in _____⁷. I work for a _____⁸ company. I go to work by _____⁹. It takes about _____¹⁰.

2 **Match the forms of transport with the places.**

	form of transport	place
1	plane	stand
2	boat/ferry	stop, station
3	bus	park
4	bicycle/bike	station, platform
5	car	airport, gate
6	train	pier

Work skills Telephoning 2

1 **Complete the telephone conversation. Write one word in each gap.**

Receiver Hello. ABC Studios. Can I _____¹ you?

Caller Could I speak to David Ellis, please?

Receiver I'm _____². He's not in the office this morning. Can I _____³ a message?

Caller Yes, please. Could you ask him to call me? My _____⁴ is Jack Freeman.

Receiver Can you _____⁵ your family name for me, please?

Caller Yes, it's F-R-E-E-M-A-N. And my office _____⁶ is 07455 672213.

Receiver Thank you, Mr Freeman.

Caller Thanks, goodbye.

2 ◀)) **5.8 Listen to the conversations. Complete the emails.**

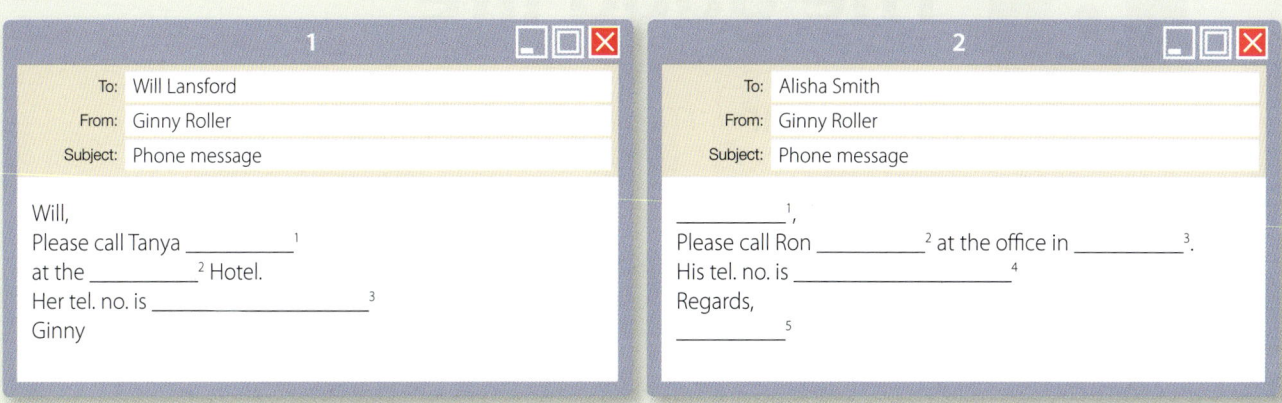

1

To:	Will Lansford
From:	Ginny Roller
Subject:	Phone message

Will,
Please call Tanya _____ [1]
at the _____ [2] Hotel.
Her tel. no. is _____ [3]
Ginny

2

To:	Alisha Smith
From:	Ginny Roller
Subject:	Phone message

_____ [1],
Please call Ron _____ [2] at the office in _____ [3].
His tel. no. is _____ [4]
Regards,
_____ [5]

Functions Talking about things you like; making suggestions

We use *like* + noun to talk about things we like.
Example   I like art and films.

We use *like* + verb *-ing* to talk about activities we like.
Example   We like going to concerts at the Royal Albert Hall.

We use *How about* + verb *-ing* or *Why don't you* + verb to make suggestions.
Examples   How about taking a tour of the city?
        Why don't you have lunch at the Spaghetti House?

PRACTICE

1 Make five sentences about things you like.
Example   I like Italian food.

2 Complete the conversations.

A Do you like sightseeing?
B Yes, _____ [1].
A OK. _____ [2] go on a guided tour?
B That's a good idea.

A Do you like sushi?
B No, _____ [3].
A Do you like tempura?
B Yes, I do.
A How about _____ [4] to a Japanese restaurant?
B Good idea.

A I like Van Gogh's paintings.
B Why _____ [5] visit the National Gallery?
A OK.

A Do you like _____ [6]?
B Yes, I do.
A Well, how _____ [7] going to Hyde Park?
B Great.

A _____ [8] music?
B Yes.
A How about _____ [9] tickets for a concert tonight?
B That's a great idea.

6 The good life

Grammar *I, me, my*

INTRODUCTION   **1**   ●)) **6.1 Listen and read the interview with Carlos and Maria Costa.**

HIGH*flyer*.co.uk

| news | blogs | pictures | sign in | search | live chat |

Join Carlos and Maria Costa online here from 10.00–12.00. Ask them about their new life in the Emirates.

Rafael   You're from Argentina. Do you live there now?

Maria   No, we don't. We live in our new home in Dubai.

Sean   Do you have a new yacht as well?

Carlos   Yes, a Volvo 60. It's beautiful – very fast and great to sail.

Angela   Have you got a sponsor for your boat?

Maria   Yes, we've got a very good sponsor. It's a TV company. We use its logo on our clothes and equipment. It's a big help for us.

Kim   Do you race every month?

Maria   Yes. Our next race is in September. It's Les Voiles de Saint-Tropez in France.

Kim   Do you have any other interests or hobbies?

Maria   We own a small fish restaurant near the Dubai Yacht Club. Carlos manages the restaurant and his father helps me in the kitchen. I really enjoy it.

Denis   It sounds like you both have a very busy lifestyle.

Carlos   Yes, that's true. But Maria also likes a quiet life. For her it's good to have her private time. In the evening, she loves to read or phone her friends and her family. She speaks with them for hours!

Maria   And Carlos sits with his friends for hours in the restaurant. He loves to talk about sailing and yachts. That's important for him!

2   ●)) **6.1 Listen again. Are the sentences true or false?**

		True	False
1	Maria and Carlos live in Dubai.	☐	☐
2	Their sponsor is a film company.	☐	☐
3	Their clothes have got the sponsor's logo on them.	☐	☐
4	Carlos manages the restaurant.	☐	☐
5	Maria's father is the chef.	☐	☐
6	They have a busy lifestyle.	☐	☐
7	Maria likes to meet her family and friends in the evening.	☐	☐

Focus

Complete the table. Find the words in the interview in 1.

Subject pronouns	I	you		she	it		
Object pronouns		you	him		it	us	
Possessive adjectives	my		his	her			their

Complete the rules. Choose the correct word.

Subject pronouns come *before / after* the verb.
Object pronouns come *before / after* the verb.
Possessive adjectives come *before / after* nouns.

⏵⏵ For more details and practice, go to the Review section on pages 62 and 63.

PRACTICE

3 Choose the correct ending for the sentences.

1   **A**   Hello. Is that you, Carlos?
    B   Yes, it's _____.   me   I

2   **A**   Where's my phone?
    B   I don't know. I can't find _____.   it   its

3   **A**   Do you like my new shoes and dress?
    B   Yes, I really like _____.   them   it

4   **A**   Does Carlos like nightclubs, Maria?
    B   No, he hates _____.   it   them

5   **A**   Does your father work in the restaurant?
    B   Yes. He really enjoys _____.   him   it

4 Complete the questions and answers.

1   Are _____ from Argentina?
    Yes, _____ am.
2   Do _____ and Maria live in the Emirates?
    Yes, _____ do.
3   Is _____ new home in Dubai?
    That's right. _____ live in Dubai now.
4   Is _____ yacht very fast?
    Yes, _____ is.
5   Have _____ got your sponsor's logo on _____ clothes?
    Yes, _____ have and _____ logos are also on the sails of _____
    yacht.
6   Does Carlos like to sit with _____ friends in _____ restaurant?
    Yes, _____ loves to sit and talk to _____.
7   What does Maria do in the evening?
    _____ phones _____ friends.
8   I would like to meet _____. When is _____ next race?
    _____'s in September. Come and meet _____ in Dubai!

5 ⏺⧙ **6.2 Listen and check your answers.**

6 Work in pairs. Practise the questions and answers in **4**.

TASK

7 Work in pairs. Talk about:

- you and your lifestyle   • a friend or colleague   • a pop group or sports team

Examples   My job is very interesting but I am always very busy.
               My friend is called Kenichi. He lives in Japan.
               I like the Boston Red Sox. They are the best team in the American
               League. I watch them on TV in Japan.

Vocabulary Food and drink

1 Match the food a–r with the words 1–18.

a
b
c
d
e
f
g
h
i
j
k
l
m
n
o
p
q
r

1 chips / French fries	___	10 couscous	___
2 burger	___	11 chicken curry	___
3 pasta	___	12 nan bread	___
4 pizza	___	13 baguette	___
5 soup	___	14 croissant	___
6 salad	___	15 oranges	___
7 rice	___	16 bananas	___
8 noodles	___	17 tiramisu	___
9 kebabs	___	18 ice cream	___

2 ◆)) **6.3** Listen and repeat.

3 Work in pairs. Ask and answer questions about things you eat.

    Example   **A** Do you like European food, Siu Lin?
                    B Yes, I do. I like Italian food so I eat lots of pasta, like spaghetti with meat sauce.

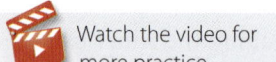 Watch the video for more practice.

Work skills Travelling and money

1 Match the countries a–h with the currencies 1–8.

a the European Union   b the USA   c China   d India

e Brazil   f Japan   g the UAE   h the UK

1	yen	___	4	euro	___	7	yuan	___
2	real	___	5	dirham	___	8	dollar	___
3	rupee	___	6	pound	___			

2 ◉) 6.4 Listen and check your answers.

3 ◉) 6.5 Listen. Maria Costa is going to Paris. She asks a friend about the trip.

Maria	Is Paris expensive?
Daniel	Yes, it is. Prices are very high in the tourist areas.
Maria	How much is a hotel?
Daniel	Cheap hotels near the airport cost about 90 euros. Good hotels in the centre of Paris cost around 170 euros a night. Luxury hotels cost over 200 euros.
Maria	I'd like to stay in a good hotel, I think. How much is the flight?
Daniel	A return flight from Dubai to Paris is about 3,000 dirham.
Maria	And how much is a taxi from Charles de Gaulle Airport to the city?
Daniel	It's between 40 and 70 euros.
Maria	How about food?
Daniel	It's pretty expensive. About 40 euros for a lunch menu.
Maria	OK. Can I get internet access?
Daniel	No problem. Wi-Fi is free in a lot of places in Paris.
Maria	Great. Is the exchange rate good?
Daniel	I'm not sure. I think 10 dirham is about 2 euros.
Maria	Right. Thanks for your help.

4 Complete the details. Use the information from 3.

Travel details

Name	Maria _____ ¹
Date	14–15 April
Journey	Dubai to _____ ²

Expenses	Details	Cost in euros
Flight	Return ticket	_____ 3
Taxi	Airport to city centre	_____ 4 x2
Eating out	One meal	_____ 5
Hotel	One night	_____ 6
Wi-Fi		_____ 7
Exchange rate	10 dirham = € _____ 8	

5 Work in pairs. Ask and answer about a city you know.

Example A Is São Paulo expensive?
B No, it isn't.
A How much is a hotel?

Functions Eating out

INTRODUCTION

1 ●) **6.6** Helen Moran invites an important customer, Silvio Rivera, to dinner. First she makes a reservation. Read and listen to the conversation.

Restaurant	Bocca di Leone. How can I help you?
Helen	I'd like to make a reservation for tonight, please.
Restaurant	Certainly. For how many people?
Helen	For two.
Restaurant	For two people. And from what time?
Helen	Seven thirty.
Restaurant	Seven thirty. And your name, please?
Helen	Yes, it's Helen Moran. M-O-R-A-N.
Restaurant	Thank you very much, Ms Moran. We'll see you at 7.30.
Helen	Thank you.

2 ●) **6.6** Listen again. Complete the reservation details.

Restaurant	_____ 1
Customer name	_____ 2
Time	_____ 3
Number of guests	_____ 4

3 Practise the conversation in **1**. Use your own name.

4 ●) **6.7** Helen and Silvio arrive at the restaurant. Listen and tick ✓ the things they order.

	Soup	Salad	Pasta	Pizza	Water	Orange juice
Helen						
Silvio						

5 ●) **6.8** Listen to Helen and Silvio. Choose the correct option.

1 Silvio's soup is   OK / very tasty.
2 Helen's salad is   OK / delicious.
3 Helen's pasta is   pretty good / very tasty.
4 Silvio's pizza is   OK / really good.
5 Their meal is   pretty good / really good.

PRACTICE

6 Order the conversation.

A Certainly. For how many people?   ___

B Yes, it's Kate Osbourne. O-S-B-O-U-R-N-E.   ___

B Eight o'clock this evening.   ___

A How can I help you?   *1*

A Thank you very much, Ms Osbourne. We'll see you at 8.00. ___

B I'd like to make a reservation, please.   ___

B For eight.   ___

B Thank you.   ___

A Eight o'clock. And your name, please?   ___

A For eight people. And from what time?   ___

7 Who asks the questions?

		Waiter	Guests	
1	Are you ready to order?	☐	☐	___
2	Do you have any vegetarian dishes?	☐	☐	___
3	And what would you like to drink?	☐	☐	___
4	Can we have some bread and olives, please?	☐	☐	___
5	How's your soup, Fiona?	☐	☐	___
6	How was your meal? Was everything OK?	☐	☐	___
7	Would you like a dessert, madam?	☐	☐	___
8	Could we have the bill, please?	☐	☐	___

8 Match the answers a–h with the questions in 7.

a Yes, we have a tofu and vegetable curry.

b Certainly. Would you like to pay by credit card?

c Of course. Would you like white or brown bread?

d It's pretty good.

e A bottle of water and a glass of orange juice, please.

f Could you give us a moment, please?

g Not for me, thanks.

h It was very good, thank you.

TASK

9 Work in pairs. Make a reservation. Use these details.

Restaurant	Zafferano Restaurant
Day	tomorrow
Number of guests	4
Time	8.30
Customer name	your name

10 Work in groups of three. Order a meal. Go to page 107.

Review

Grammar *I, me, my*

Form

Subject pronouns

I   you   he   she   it   we   they
Subject pronouns go before the verb in positive statements.
Example   He has got a yacht.

Subject pronouns go between the auxiliary verb and the main verb in questions.
Example   Do they have any sponsors?

Object pronouns

me   you   him   her   it   us   them
Object pronouns go after the verb in positive statements and questions.
Examples   Maria always races with me.
              Do you like it?

Subject	Verb	Object
Tamsin (She)	likes	William (him).
Jack (He)	loves	Masha (her).
Tania and Nikki (They)	like	Greg and Sven (them).

Object pronouns go after prepositions and after the verb *be*.
Examples   He sails with her.
              Is that a problem for you?
              A Who's that on the yacht?   B It's me.

Possessive adjectives

my   your   his   her   its   our   their
Possessive adjectives go before nouns.
Examples   My husband manages the restaurant.
              Where's your home now?
              His father helps in the kitchen.

Use

We use pronouns to refer to people, things, and actions. We also use pronouns to give short answers.
Examples   We've got a new Volvo 60 racing yacht. It's beautiful.
              A Do you enjoy working in the restaurant with Carlos?
              B Yes, I love it.

PRACTICE   **1 Match the pairs of sentences, 1–6 with a–f.**

1	She loves him.	a	Carlos loves talking about sailing.
2	He loves her.	b	Maria loves Carlos.
3	They love it.	c	Zayed and his wife love their children.
4	She loves them.	d	Joachim loves his wife.
5	They love them.	e	Carlos and Maria love their new yacht.
6	He loves it.	f	Joachim's wife loves the big shopping malls.

2 **Choose the correct word.**

1 This is Carlos' hat. Could you give it to *him / his*?

2 Our new yacht is a Volvo. *It's / Its* 19 metres long and *it's / its* mast is 10 metres high.

3 *You're / Your* from Argentina but *you're / your* house is in the Emirates.

4 Carlos talks to *he's / his* father in the kitchen and *he's / his* always happy when they work together.

5 Could you give *me / my you / your* telephone number?

3 **Replace the highlighted nouns with pronouns.**

Joachim   Have you got any children, Zayed?

Zayed   Yes, I have.

Joachim   Can you tell me about **your children** _____ [1]?

Zayed   Well, I've got a son. His name is Mohammed.

Joachim   How old is **Mohammed** _____ [2]?

Zayed   **Mohammed** _____ [3] is almost twelve.

Joachim   And do you have any other children?

Zayed   Yes, I've got two daughters.

Joachim   And what are **your daughters** _____ [4] called?

Zayed   **My daughters** _____ [5] are called Seda and Mona.

Joachim   How old is Seda?

Zayed   **Seda** _____ [6] is eight.

Joachim   And how old is her sister?

Zayed   **Her sister** _____ [7] is nine years old.

Joachim   Do you and your wife have a busy lifestyle?

Zayed   Not really. **My wife and I** _____ [8] have a very simple lifestyle.

4 **Complete the sentences.**

My wife and I live near the Dubai yacht club. _____ [1] apartment is quite big. _____ [2] have three children. _____ [3] son Raphael has _____ [4] own room. _____ [5] daughters share a bedroom, but they have _____ [6] own bathroom.

5 **Make the second question the same as the first.**

1 Does this yacht belong to you?	Is this _____ yacht?
2 Is this Maria's phone?	Is this _____ phone?
3 Does this yacht club belong to the members?	Is it _____ club?
4 Do you think this money belongs to us?	Do you think it's _____ money?
5 Is this Zayed's car?	Is this _____ car?

Vocabulary Food and drink

1 **Label the pictures.**

1 _____ 2 _____ 3 _____ 4 _____ 5 _____

6 _____ 7 _____ 8 _____ 9 _____ 10 _____

2 ◗) **6.9** **Listen to Yasmina from the Emirates. She is talking about the food she eats. Are the sentences true or false?**

		True	False
1	She has breakfast at 7.30.	☐	☐
2	She drinks coffee for breakfast.	☐	☐
3	She eats rice with eggs for breakfast.	☐	☐
4	She has lunch in the office at one o'clock.	☐	☐
5	She eats meat for lunch.	☐	☐
6	She goes to a restaurant with friends for dinner.	☐	☐
7	She likes cooking.	☐	☐
8	She has ice cream and pastry for dessert.	☐	☐

Work skills Travelling and money

Read the information about travel expenses in Madrid. Complete the conversation.

Travel expenses in Madrid

Expenses	Details	Cost in euros
Hotel Ritz Madrid	standard room rate	570
La Moraleja Hotel	standard room rate	120
Hotel Praga	standard room rate	48
Flight	direct return	180
Taxi	airport to city	26
Wi-Fi	cafés	0
Restaurant	lunch menu	8–12
Exchange rate	£1 = €1.2	

Rebecca	Is Madrid expensive?
Daniel	It's not so expensive.
Rebecca	How much is a hotel?
Daniel	Cheap hotels cost about _____[1] euros. Good hotels in the centre of Madrid cost around _____[2] euros a night. Luxury hotels cost over _____[3].
Rebecca	I'd like to stay in a good hotel, I think. How much is the flight?
Daniel	A return flight from London to Madrid is about _____[4].
Rebecca	And how much is a taxi from Madrid-Barajas Airport to the city?
Daniel	It's about _____[5].
Rebecca	Is there internet access outside the office?
Daniel	No problem. Wi-Fi is _____[6] in a lot of cafés in Madrid.
Rebecca	Is food expensive?
Daniel	No, it's quite cheap. A lunch menu is between _____[7] and _____[8].
Rebecca	Great. Is the exchange rate good?
Daniel	I'm not sure. I think one pound is _____[9].
Rebecca	Right. Thanks for your help.

Functions Eating out

> We use *I'd like* + *to* + verb to say what we want to do.
> **Example** I'd like to make a reservation, please.
>
> We use *I'll have* + (food/drink) to order from a menu.
> **Example** I'll have the vegetable curry.
>
> We use *How's ...?* to ask about the food.
> **Example** How's your pasta?

PRACTICE

1 Match the sentences 1–8 with the replies a–h.

1 I'd like to make a reservation for tomorrow, please. ___
2 Are you ready to order? ___
3 What would you like to drink? ___
4 Do you have any vegetarian dishes? ___
5 Would you like to pay by credit card or cash? ___
6 How's your risotto? ___
7 Would you like a dessert? ___
8 Can we have the bill, please? ___

a Yes, we do. We have risotto with mushroom and cheese.
b It's really good.
c Certainly. For what time?
d Sparkling mineral water for me, please.
e Yes, certainly.
f By credit card. Is AmEx OK?
g Yes. I'd like the soup, please.
h Not for me, thanks.

2 Put the sentences in 1 in the correct group.

Making a reservation	
Ordering food and drink	2g
Asking about the food and meal	
Paying	

7 High flyer

Grammar Questions: *Wh-* and *How* +

INTRODUCTION **1** 7.1 **Listen and read the interview with Shirin Nassar.**

Flying high!

This month we talk to Shirin Nassar.

Reporter So, Shirin, what kind of company do you work for?
Shirin I work for an airline.

Reporter Where is the main office?
Shirin At Doha International Airport in Qatar.

Reporter And what do you do?
Shirin I'm a cabin attendant.

Reporter Where do you fly?
Shirin I fly all around the world – New York, Shanghai, Paris, Cape Town, and so on.

Reporter Which is your favourite city?
Shirin I love Paris. It's great for shopping and restaurants and sightseeing. Everything.

Reporter How many times do you fly in a month?
Shirin It depends. About eight or ten.

Reporter And when do you have a break?
Shirin I have a break after every flight. Usually one or two days. I get a longer break after a long flight like Tokyo or Buenos Aires.

Reporter Who do you work with?
Shirin On a flight I work with a team of about ten cabin crew and three flight crew.

Reporter When is your next flight?
Shirin After this interview.

2 **Are the sentences true or false?**

		True	False
1	Shirin Nassar works for an airline company.	☐	☐
2	The main office is in Abu Dhabi.	☐	☐
3	Shirin is a pilot.	☐	☐
4	Shirin flies to Europe and Asia.	☐	☐
5	She flies once a month.	☐	☐
6	Shirin has a break after a flight.	☐	☐
7	She works with about 13 crew on a flight.	☐	☐

Focus

Complete the table with question words from the text.

Information	Question word
general facts times or dates people places numbers	*what, which*

Read the examples.

Where is the main office?

When is your next flight?

What do you do?

Where do you fly?

Complete the rules with *verb* or *subject*.

To make *Wh-* questions with *be*, we use *Wh-* + *be* + _____.

To make *Wh-* questions with *do*, we use *Wh-* + *do* + subject + _____.

Find more examples of the two types in the text.

▶▶ For more details and practice, go to the Review section on pages 72 and 73.

PRACTICE

3 **Write the questions for the sentences in 2.**

Example   What kind of company does Shirin work for?

4 **Work in pairs. Ask and answer the questions about Shirin.**

Example   **A** What does she do?

   B She's a cabin attendant.

5 **Complete the conversation with these words.**

What   When   Where   Which   How many   Who

Sylvia   Hi. I'm Sylvia.

Gordon   Hello, I'm Gordon.

Sylvia   Nice to meet you, Gordon. _____¹ company do you work for?

Gordon   I work for STN Airlines.

Sylvia   _____² do you do?

Gordon   I'm a pilot.

Sylvia   _____³ do you work?

Gordon   My base is Heathrow Airport, in London.

Sylvia   _____⁴ times do you fly in a week?

Gordon   I fly to Europe so I do two flights a day, five days a week.

Sylvia   So, about ten flights a week?

Gordon   Yes.

Sylvia   _____⁵ do you fly with?

Gordon   I fly with just one other pilot, the first officer. And of course the cabin crew.

Sylvia   _____⁶ is your next flight?

Gordon   On Saturday.

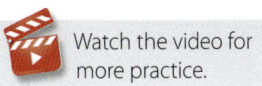
Watch the video for more practice.

6 ●)) **7.2 Listen and check your answers.**

TASK

7 **Ask other students in the class about their jobs. Go to page 106.**

Vocabulary Airports

1 Look at the plan of an airport. Match the words with the airport signs. Write the letters.

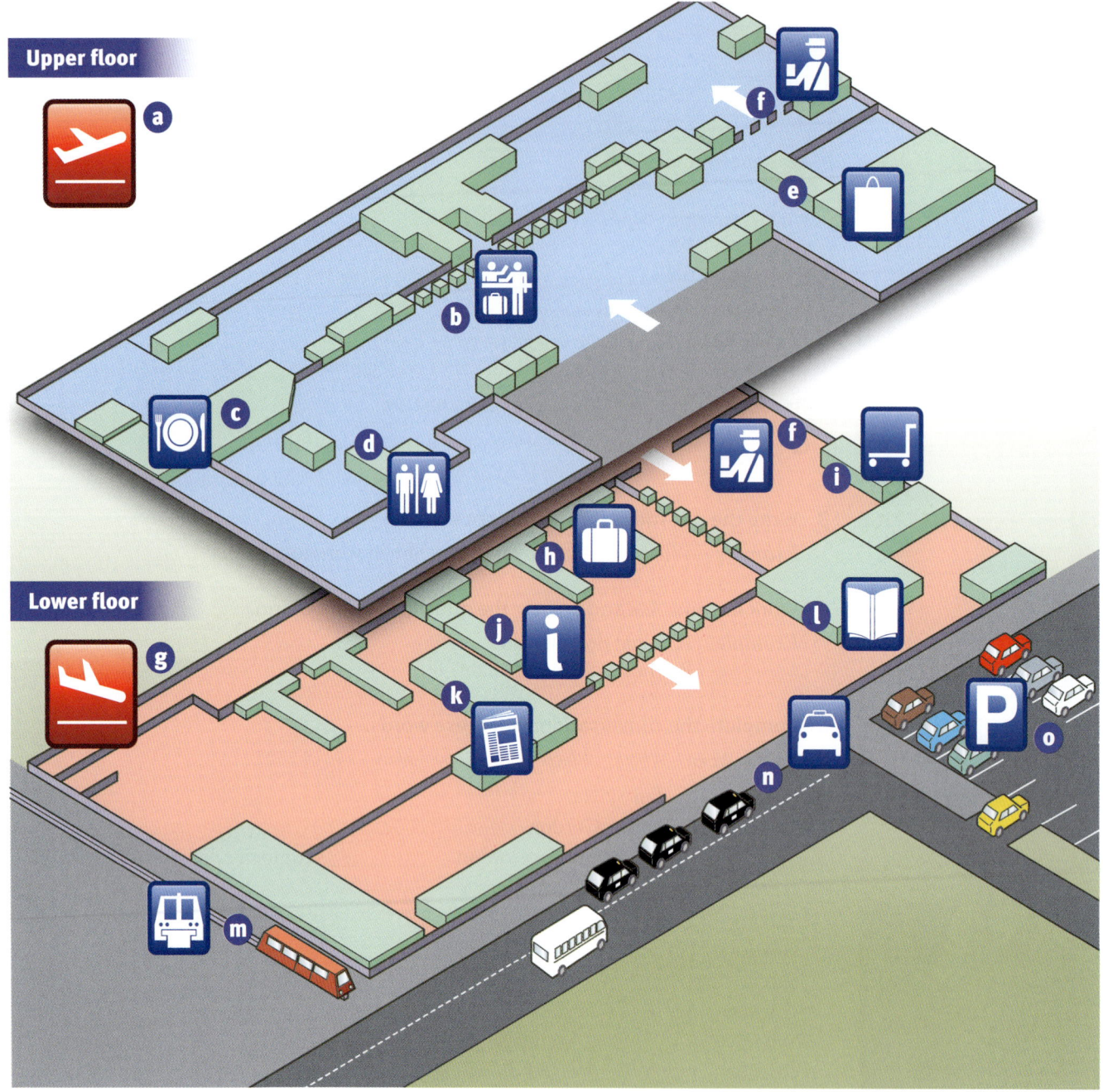

monorail	___	toilets	___	newsagent's	___
departures	___	security	___	baggage claim	___
information desk	___	taxi stand	___	bookshop	___
shops	___	restaurants	___	trolleys	___
parking	___	arrivals	___	check-in desks	___

2 •)) 7.3 Listen and repeat.

3 •)) 7.4 Listen to the voice messages. Mark the meeting points 1 to 4 on the plan in 1.

4 Work in pairs. Ask about the places in the airport.

Example A Where do people buy books?
B In the bookshop.

Work skills Emails 2

1 **Look at email 1. Is the email:**
   a   an invitation to Japan?
   b   details of travel plans?

1

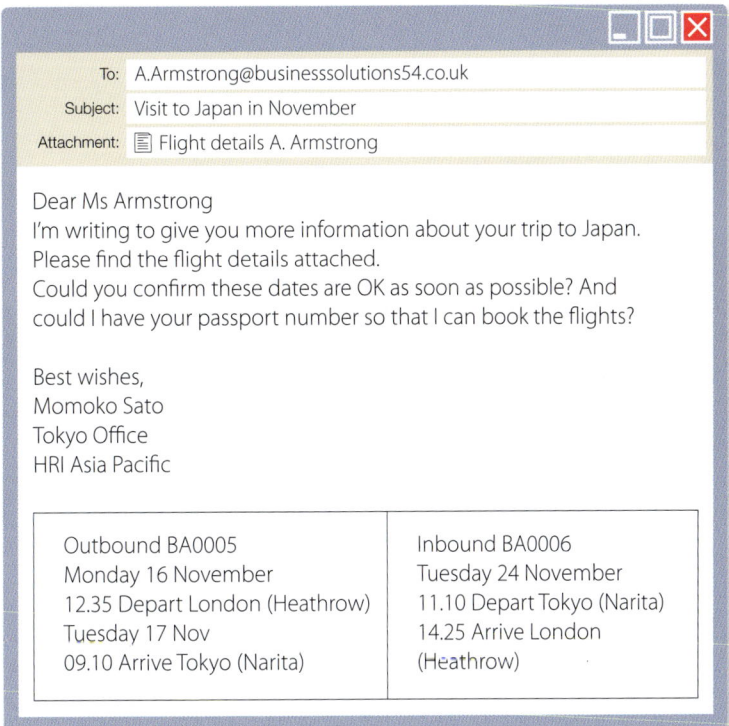

To: A.Armstrong@businesssolutions54.co.uk
Subject: Visit to Japan in November
Attachment: 📄 Flight details A. Armstrong

Dear Ms Armstrong
I'm writing to give you more information about your trip to Japan.
Please find the flight details attached.
Could you confirm these dates are OK as soon as possible? And
could I have your passport number so that I can book the flights?

Best wishes,
Momoko Sato
Tokyo Office
HRI Asia Pacific

Outbound BA0005	Inbound BA0006
Monday 16 November	Tuesday 24 November
12.35 Depart London (Heathrow)	11.10 Depart Tokyo (Narita)
Tuesday 17 Nov	14.25 Arrive London
09.10 Arrive Tokyo (Narita)	(Heathrow)

2

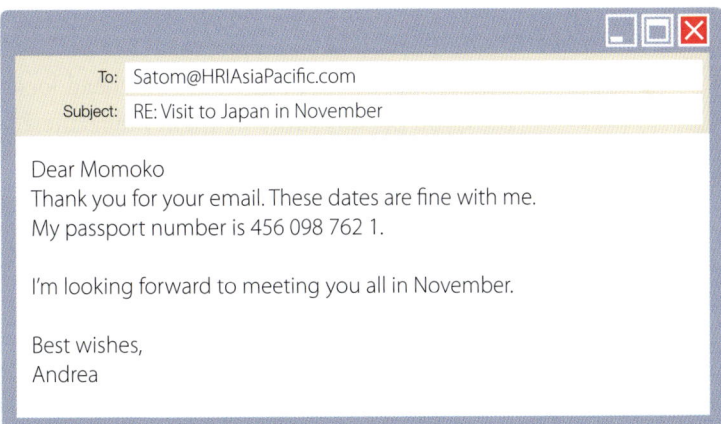

To: Satom@HRIAsiaPacific.com
Subject: RE: Visit to Japan in November

Dear Momoko
Thank you for your email. These dates are fine with me.
My passport number is 456 098 762 1.

I'm looking forward to meeting you all in November.

Best wishes,
Andrea

2 **Read emails 1 and 2. Find the sentence that:**
   1   explains why Momoko is writing the email. _____
   2   explains that there is an attachment. _____
   3   asks Andrea to do something. _____
   4   asks Andrea to send something to Momoko. _____
   5   thanks Momoko for her email. _____
   6   answers Momoko's question. _____
   7   gives the information Momoko asks for. _____

3 **Student A, go to page 106. Student B, go to page 108.**

Functions Making requests

1 **Find these things in the picture.**

1	seat ___	5	window blind ___
2	safety belt ___	6	blanket ___
3	folding table ___	7	lights ___
4	overhead locker ___	8	remote control ___

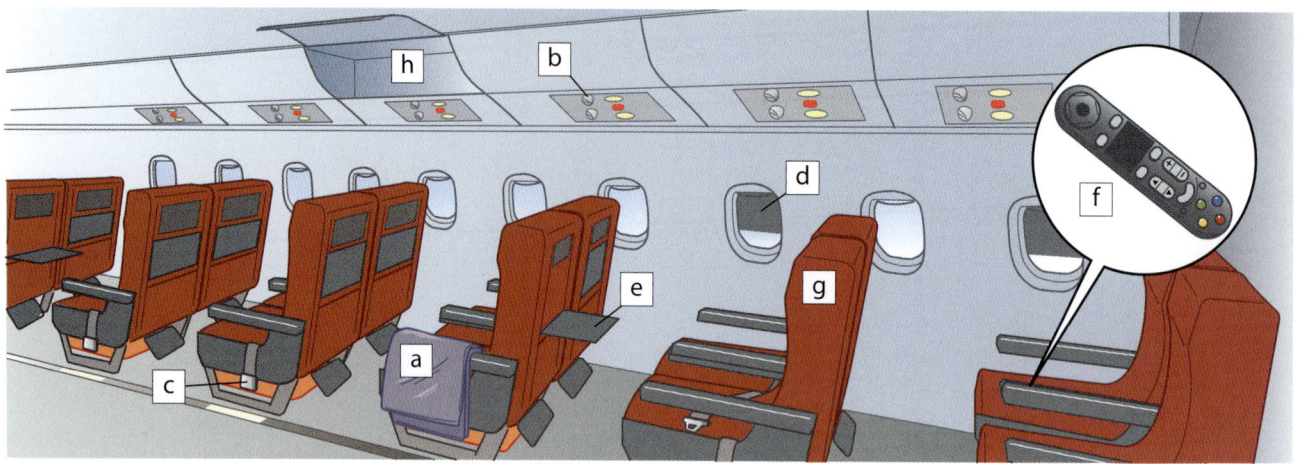

2 •)) **7.5** **Listen and repeat.**

3 •)) **7.6** **Listen. Does the cabin attendant or passenger make the requests? Put the requests in the correct group.**

1 Could you close your window blind, please?
2 Could I have the pasta, please? And could I have another tomato juice?
3 Could you show me how to use the remote control?
4 Could you fasten your safety belt?
5 Could I have a blanket, please?
6 Could you put your bag in the overhead locker?
7 Have you got any more in-flight magazines?
8 Could you go back to your seat, please, sir?

Cabin attendant	Passenger

4 **Match the words 1–5 with the pictures a–e.**

1 boarding card ___
2 menu ___
3 landing card ___
4 in-flight magazine ___
5 safety card ___

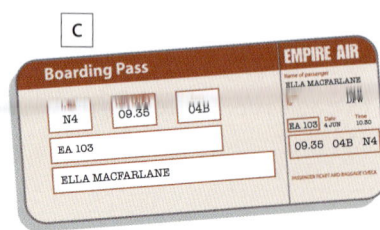

Focus

Read the examples and complete the table.

Could you close your window blind, please?
Could I have the pasta, please?
Could you put your bag in the overhead locker?
Have you got any more in-flight magazines?

The speaker wants X	The speaker wants the listener to do X

Complete the rules.

We use _____ to ask someone to do something.
We use _____ or _____ to ask for something.
We use *Sure, OK,* and *Certainly* to give a *positive / negative* answer.

▶ For more details and practice, go to the Review section on page 75.

PRACTICE

5 Complete the conversations with these phrases.

Could you   Could I   Have you got   Could I   Could you   Could you

1 A Good evening. _____ see your boarding card, please?
   B Here you are.
   A Thank you. You're in row 15.

2 A _____ put your bag under the seat, please?
   B OK.

3 A Sorry. _____ have a glass of mineral water?
   B Certainly, sir. With ice?
   A Yes, please.

4 A _____ go back to your seat and fasten your safety belt?
   B Sure. Could I get my sweater first?
   A OK.

5 A _____ any more menus?
   B Yes. I'll bring you one in just a moment.

6 A _____ check my folding table? I think it's broken.
   B OK. I'll ask the Chief Purser to look at it for you.

6 ◉) 7.7 Listen and check your answers.

7 Work in pairs. Practise the conversations in 5.

TASK

8 Work in pairs. Role-play these situations.

The passenger wants a safety card.
The cabin attendant wants the passenger to fasten their safety belt.
The passenger wants a blanket.
The cabin attendant wants the passenger to sit down.
The passenger wants a landing card.

Review

Grammar Questions: *Wh-* and *How* +

Form

To make *Wh-* questions with *be*, we use *Wh-* + *be* + subject.
Example **A** Where is Qatar? **B** It's in the Middle East.

To make *Wh-* questions with *do*, we use *Wh-* + *do* + subject + verb.
Example **A** Where does Qatar Airlines fly? **B** It flies all over the world.

Use

We use *Wh-* question words for 'open' questions. We sometimes call these 'information' or 'content' questions.

We use *where* to ask about places.
Example **A** Where do you live? **B** I live in Edinburgh.

We use *when* to ask about a time or a date.
Example **A** When is the conference? **B** It's in November.

We use *what* or *which* to ask for general facts.
Example **A** What do you do? **B** I work for a charity.

We use *who* to ask about a person or people.
Example **A** Who do you work with?
             B I have three colleagues in my department.

We use *how many* to talk about numbers.
Example **A** How many people work on an aeroplane? **B** About 15.

PRACTICE

1 Read the answers and complete the questions.

1	_____ is he?	He's my business partner.
2	_____ is the meeting?	On Monday, at 10.00.
3	_____ is the conference?	It's in New York.
4	_____ rooms has the hotel got?	It's got 570 rooms.
5	_____ is the conference about?	Global marketing.
6	_____ people are going to the conference?	About 5,000.

2 Make *Wh-* questions.

1 (she) what / study? _____
2 (they) where / work? _____
3 (you) when / start work? _____
4 (he) what time / finish work? _____
5 (she) who / work for? _____
6 (the train) when / arrive? _____
7 (it) what time / leave? _____
8 (they) what / want? _____
9 when / be / your birthday? _____
10 where / be / Barcelona? _____

3 Write the answers.

1 Who do you work for? _____
2 Where are you based? _____
3 What qualifications have you got? _____
4 How many people work for your company? _____
5 How many languages do you speak? _____
6 What time do you start work? _____
7 When do you finish work? _____
8 How many conferences do you go to a year? _____

4 Order the conversation.

Sally	Hi, I'm Sally.	_1_
Jaime	I work for Logun Ltd.	___
Sally	Where is Bordeaux?	___
Sally	Ah yes. Is Bordeaux big? How many people live there?	___
Sally	Nice to meet you too. Who do you work for, Jaime?	___
Sally	I live in Birmingham, in the UK.	___
Jaime	About 100,000. What about you, Sally? Where do you live?	___
Sally	Oh, and where is Logun Ltd based?	___
Jaime	In Bordeaux.	___
Jaime	It's in France.	___
Jaime	Hi, I'm Jaime. Nice to meet you.	___

5 Aneta Karlowicz has an unusual job. Match the questions 1–7 with the answers a–g. What is Aneta's job?

1 Who do you meet in your job? ___
2 What do you do? ___
3 Where is your next assignment? ___
4 When do you work? ___
5 Which is your favourite country? ___
6 How many hotels do you visit a year? ___
7 Where do you work? ___

a I love Thailand. The food and culture are amazing.
b I probably visit about a hundred hotels.
c I visit hotels all around the world.
d I work morning, afternoon, and night.
e I meet hotel guests and staff.
f I work in many different countries and I work in many different hotels.
g A resort in the Maldive Islands. I'm really looking forward to it.

Vocabulary Airports

Look at the pictures. Complete the crossword.

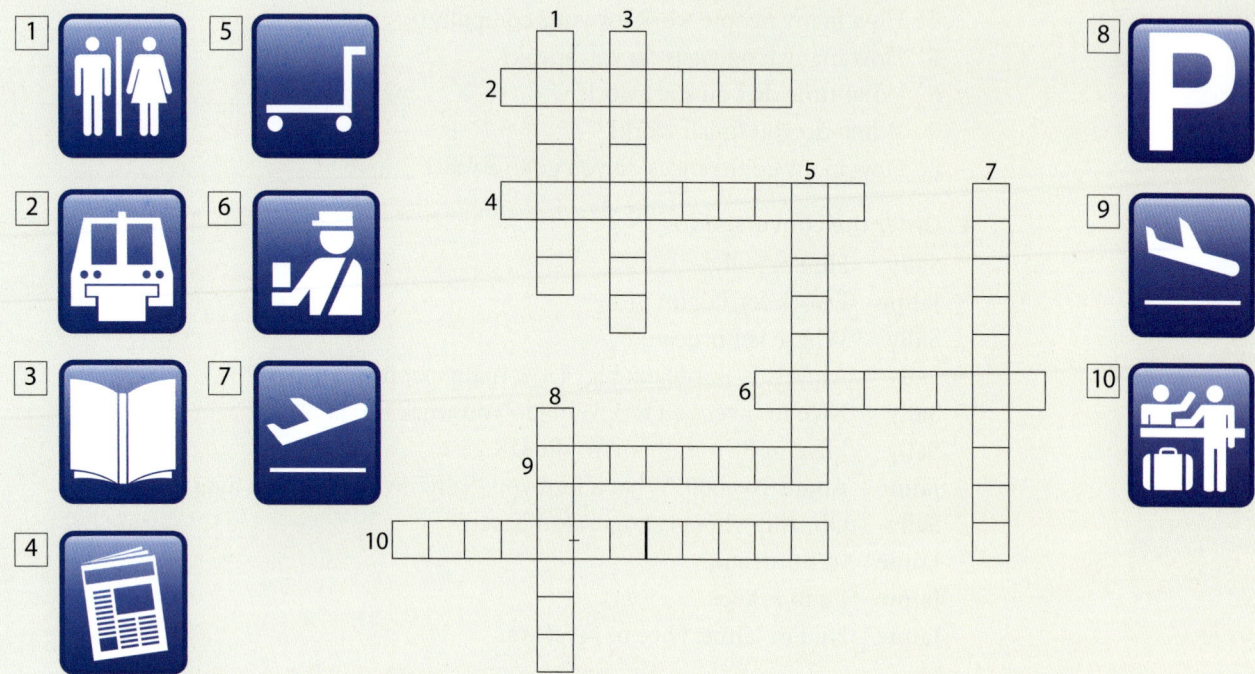

Work skills Emails 2

1 **Read Laurent's reply to an email from David.**

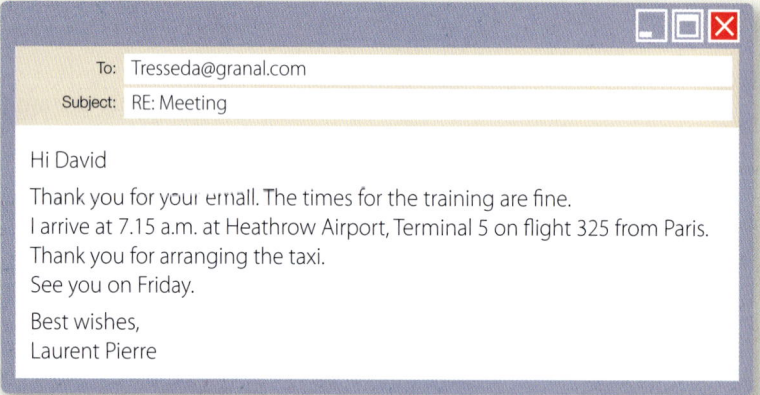

To: Tresseda@granal.com
Subject: RE: Meeting

Hi David
Thank you for your email. The times for the training are fine.
I arrive at 7.15 a.m. at Heathrow Airport, Terminal 5 on flight 325 from Paris.
Thank you for arranging the taxi.
See you on Friday.

Best wishes,
Laurent Pierre

2 **Complete David's email to Laurent.**

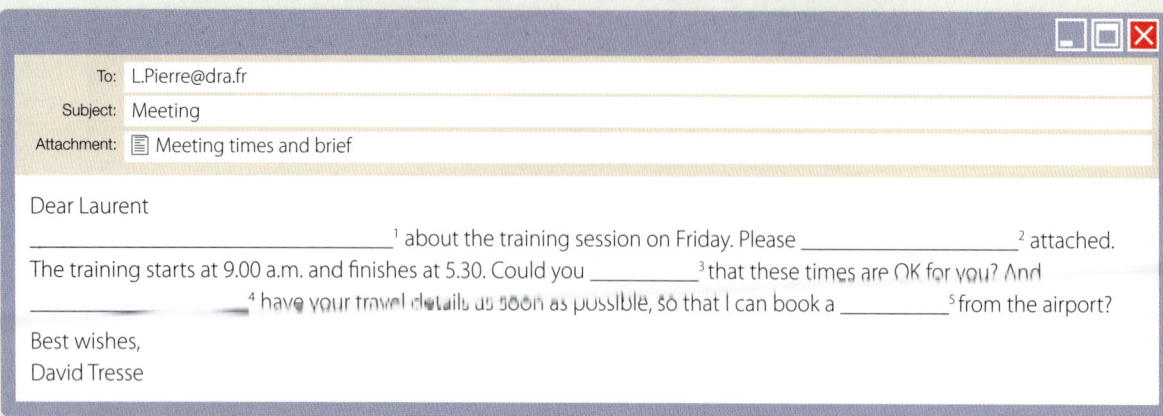

To: L.Pierre@dra.fr
Subject: Meeting
Attachment: 📄 Meeting times and brief

Dear Laurent
_____ [1] about the training session on Friday. Please _____ [2] attached.
The training starts at 9.00 a.m. and finishes at 5.30. Could you _____ [3] that these times are OK for you? And
_____ [4] have your travel details as soon as possible, so that I can book a _____ [5] from the airport?

Best wishes,
David Tresse

Functions Making requests

We use *Could I …?* to ask for something.

We use *Could you …?* to ask someone to do something.

Examples Could I have the pasta, please?

Could you close your window blind, please?

We also use *Have you got …?* to ask for something.

Example Have you got any more in-flight magazines?

We use *Sure, OK,* and *Certainly* to give a positive answer. We can also say *No problem* or *Of course.*

We usually say *…, please* at the end of *Could I …?* and *Could you …?* sentences.

When someone asks for something, we can say *Here you are* or *Here it is.*

Example A Could I have a glass of water, please?

B Here you are.

PRACTICE

Complete these conversations at the airport.

Check-in

A Good morning, madam. Welcome to Travel Air.

B Thank you.

A _____ _____ [1] see your passport and ticket, please?

B Yes, _____ _____ _____ [2].

A _____ _____ [3] put your suitcase on the scales for me?

B _____ [4].

A Thank you.

B _____ _____ [5] have a luggage tag, please?

A Certainly, madam. And here's your boarding card. Enjoy your flight.

Passport control

A _____ [6] I see your passport, please?

B Yes, here you are.

A Thank you. And your landing card, please.

B Yes, _____ [7] it is.

A OK. _____ _____ [8] look at the camera, please?

B Sure.

Customs

A Is this your bag, sir?

B Yes, it is.

A _____ _____ [9] open your bag for me, please?

B Yes, _____ [10] course.

A Thank you. That's fine.

8 Living in the past

Grammar Past Simple: *be*; regular verbs

INTRODUCTION **1** Match the names 1–4 with the pictures a–d.

1 Marilyn Monroe ___
2 Fred Astaire ___
3 The Beatles ___
4 Frank Sinatra ___

2 ◉) **8.1** Listen and read about the Savoy Hotel. How many people from **1** can you find?

The Savoy Hotel opened in London about 120 years ago. It was the first luxury hotel in England. Many famous people and celebrities stayed there. Elizabeth Taylor, Charlie Chaplin, and the Beatles were all guests.

The first famous guest was the French artist, Monet. He painted pictures of the River Thames from his hotel room. Oscar Wilde, the Irish writer, lived in the hotel for about a month. Fred Astaire danced on the roof of the hotel. Frank Sinatra played the piano in the American Bar. In the 60s, Bob Dylan stayed there and made a music video next to the hotel.

3 Read the text in **2** again. Are the sentences true or false?

		True	False
1	The Savoy Hotel was the first luxury hotel in England.	☐	☐
2	The Beatles stayed at the hotel.	☐	☐
3	Monet painted the hotel.	☐	☐
4	Famous Hollywood stars were guests at the hotel.	☐	☐
5	Frank Sinatra played the piano in the hotel restaurant.	☐	☐

4 ◉) **8.2** Listen to an interview with one of the staff from the new Savoy Hotel. Choose the best answers.

1 Did the hotel have electric lifts? Yes, it did. / No, it didn't.
2 Did famous people and royalty stay here? Yes, they did. / No, they didn't.
3 How many husbands did Elizabeth Taylor stay with? She stayed with one husband / four husbands.
4 Did Queen Elizabeth stay at the hotel? Yes, she did. / No, she didn't.
5 When did the hotel close? It closed in 2001 / 2007.
6 How much did the upgrade cost? It cost 22 / 220 million pounds.
7 When did the hotel open again? It opened in 2010 / 2011.

Focus

Read the examples.

The Savoy Hotel in London **opened** in 1889.
The first famous guest **was** the French artist, Monet.
Elizabeth Taylor, Charlie Chaplin, and the Beatles **were** all guests.

Complete the rules.

To make the Past Simple for regular verbs, we add _____ to the end of the verb.
To make the Past Simple of *be*, we use *I / you / we / they were* and *he / she / it* _____.

Read the examples.

Did famous people and royalty stay here?	Yes, they **did**.
Did the Queen stay here?	No, she **didn't**.
When **did** the hotel close?	It closed in 2007.

Complete the rules.

To make a question in the Past Simple, we use _____ + subject + verb.
To make positive short answers, we use _____.
To make negative short answers, we use _____.
To make a *Wh-* question in the Past Simple, we use *Wh-* + _____ + subject + verb.

▶▶ For more details and practice, go to the Review section on pages 82 and 83.

Watch the video for more practice.

PRACTICE

5 Write the verbs in the Past Simple.

1 open _____ 3 paint _____ 5 dance _____ 7 visit _____
2 stay _____ 4 live _____ 6 play _____ 8 be _____

6 Read the text in **2** again. Check your answers to **5**.

7 Complete the answers about the Savoy Hotel.

1	When did the Savoy Hotel open?	It _____ in 1889.
2	What did Monet do?	He _____ pictures of the River Thames.
3	How long did Oscar Wilde live in the hotel?	He _____ there for a month.
4	Did Charlie Chaplin stay at the hotel?	Yes, he _____.
5	What did Fred Astaire do?	He _____ on the roof of the hotel.
6	What happened in the American Bar?	Frank Sinatra _____ the piano.
7	Did the Beatles play at the hotel?	_____, they _____.

8 Work in pairs. Ask and answer the questions in **7**.

9 Complete the text about a famous hotel in the USA. Change the verbs in brackets into the Past Simple.

The Waldorf-Astoria is a famous hotel in New York. It _____ ¹ (open) in 1897 and _____ ² (be) the first hotel with room service. It was also the world's first skyscraper hotel. William Waldorf Astor built the original hotel.

The hotel chef, Oscar Tschirky, _____ ³ (create) the famous Waldorf Salad made from apple, nuts, celery, and mayonnaise. George Boldt _____ ⁴ (manage) the hotel and he also _____ ⁵ (introduce) Thousand Island salad dressing.

Many famous people _____ ⁶ (stay) at the hotel, including Princess Grace of Monaco, Winston Churchill, the King of Thailand, the composer Cole Porter, and President J.F. Kennedy. Marilyn Monroe _____ ⁷ (live) in the hotel for several months when she made a film in New York, *The Seven Year Itch*. Many films _____ ⁸ (use) the hotel as a location, including the comedy *Weekend at the Waldorf*.

TASK 10 Work in pairs. Student A, go to page 106. Student B, go to page 109.

Vocabulary Hotels

1 **Match the words 1–8 with the pictures a–h.**

1	reception	___	5	registration form	___
2	bags	___	6	reservation	___
3	key card	___	7	passport	___
4	credit card	___	8	lift	___

2 ●)) **8.3 Listen and repeat.**

3 **Complete the sentences with these words.**

passport   lift   reservation   key card
bags   reception   registration form   credit card

1 You make a _____ by email or by phone.
2 You go to _____ to check in.
3 You fill in the _____ and you show your _____
   and _____.
4 Reception gives you a _____ for your hotel room.
5 You take the _____ to go up to your room.
6 You or a porter carry your _____.

4 **Look at the hotel room. Match the words 1–10 with the things a–j in the rooms.**

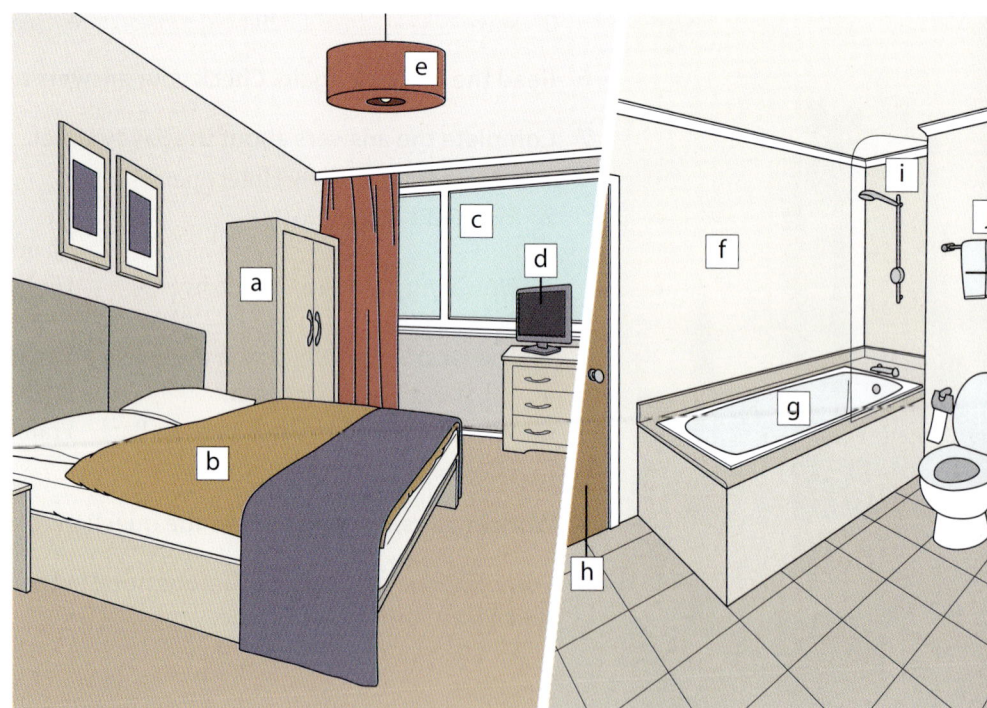

1	bed	___	5	light	___	9	towel	___
2	television	___	6	bathroom	___	10	door	___
3	wardrobe	___	7	bath	___			
4	window	___	8	shower	___			

5 ●)) **8.4 Listen and repeat.**

6 **Match the verbs with the nouns.**

Example open the door

VERBS	open	have	turn on	
NOUNS	bath	television	shower	door
	window	light	wardrobe	

Work skills Giving and checking information

1 Read the email. Answer the questions.

From: Hotel Maurice
Subject: Booking confirmation

Dear Ms Scot
Here is confirmation of your booking:

Guest name	Millena Scot
Confirmation number	89907
Arrival date	Monday 15th August
Departure date	Wednesday 17th August
Room type	Standard single
Room rate per night	250 euros

Please check through all of the above details and if anything is incorrect, please contact us on 33 1 44 58 11 11. For further information on the hotel or the local area, please visit our website: www.hotelmaurice.com.
We look forward to welcoming you to the Hotel Maurice.

---

1 What is the guest's name? _____
2 How many nights is she staying? _____
3 Is she staying in a single or double room? _____
4 How much will she pay? _____

2 ●)) 8.5 Listen. Change the information in the email in 1.

3 ●)) 8.6 Listen and complete the phrases.

A Could I _____¹ your name, please?
B Milena Scott.
A I'm sorry. Could you _____² that, please?
B Milena Scott.
A Is that with _____³ 'l's?
B No, one 'l'.
A M-I-L-E-N-A.
B That's _____⁴.

A A double room is 315 euros per night. Is that OK?
B I'm sorry, is that _____⁵ or _____⁶?
A That's 315.

B I'm sorry, it's a bit noisy. Could you _____⁷, please?
A Yes, your new confirmation number is 89917.

4 Work in pairs. Practise the conversations in 3.

5 Work in pairs. Change the details for your hotel reservation. Student B, go to page 108.

Student A You are the guest. Give your details to Student B.

Guest name	Jenny Austin	Departure date	6th March
Confirmation number	552739	Room type	Double
Arrival date	5th March	Room rate per night	216 euros

Example **Student B** Could I have your name, please?
          You   Yes, it's …

Functions Checking in and out of a hotel

INTRODUCTION

1 🔊 **8.7 Listen. A guest checks in at a hotel. Match the two parts of the conversation.**

1 How can I help you?
2 Could I have your name, please?
3 You have a double room for three nights. Is that correct?
4 Do you have your passport and credit card?
5 You're in room 306 on the third floor. Here is your key card.
6 Have you got any bags?
7 Would you like the porter to take them to your room?
8 Is there a lift?

a No, that's OK.
b Yes, I've got two.
c I'd like to check in, please.
d Yes, it's over there on the right.
e It's Rachael Young.
f Yes. Here you are.
g Yes, that's right.
h Thanks.

2 Work in pairs. Practise the parts of the conversation in 1.

3 🔊 **8.8 Rachael is checking out of the hotel. Listen and read the conversation.**

Reception	Good morning. Can I help you?
Rachael	Yes, I'd like to check out, please. Room 306.
Reception	Ms Young?
Rachael	That's right.
Reception	Have you got your key card, Ms Young?
Rachael	Of course. Here it is.
Reception	Did you use your minibar?
Rachael	Yes, I had a mineral water last night.
Reception	OK. One moment. Yes, here's your bill. How would you like to pay?
Rachael	Credit card, please.
Reception	Of course.
Rachael	Here's my card.
Reception	Thank you. Can you check the amount and enter your pin number?
Rachael	Yes, sure.
Reception	Thank you. And here's your receipt. Goodbye, Ms Young. See you again soon we hope.
Rachael	Thank you. Goodbye.

4 Read the conversation in 3 again. Are the sentences true or false?

	True	False
1 Rachael was in room 306.	☐	☐
2 Rachael doesn't have her key card.	☐	☐
3 Rachael had a drink from the minibar.	☐	☐
4 Rachael wants to pay by credit card.	☐	☐
5 Rachael can't remember her pin number.	☐	☐

Focus

Complete the table with these phrases.

Have you got your key card?

Have you got any bags?

Would you like the porter to take it to your room?

Here is your key card.

Can you please check the amount and enter your pin?

I'd like to check out, please.

I'd like to check in.

Here's your bill.

Is there a lift?

Here's your receipt.

You are in room 306.

How would you like to pay?

Checking in	Checking out

▶ For more details and practice, go to the Review section on page 85.

PRACTICE

5 ◉》 **8.9** Listen to the conversation at reception. Fill in the details.

1 Name _____
2 Number of nights _____
3 Room type _____
4 Room number _____
5 Floor _____

6 Practise the conversation in **3**. Use this information.

Room 511
Name your real name
Minibar tomato juice
Payment by cash

TASK

7 Work in pairs. Practise the conversation.

Reception	Guest
Good morning / afternoon / evening.	Good morning / afternoon / evening. I'd like to check in.
Could I have your name, please?	Give your name.
Is it a single / double room for one night / two nights?	Yes, that's right.
Could you fill in the registration form, please?	Yes, of course.
Do you have your passport and a credit card?	Yes, here you are.
Thanks. Here's your key card, Mr / Ms _____.	
You're in room 104 / 204 / 304. That's on the ground / first / second floor.	Thank you. Where are the stairs / lifts, please?
On the right / left. Enjoy your stay.	Thank you.

Review

Grammar Past Simple: *be*; regular verbs

Form

Regular verbs in the Past Simple

To make the Past Simple of regular verbs, we add *-ed* to the end of the verb.
Examples The hotel opened in 1889.
Fred Astaire danced on the roof.

The *-ed* ending is pronounced in three different ways.

/d/	/t/	/ɪd/
lived	danced	started

●)) 8.10 **Listen and repeat the *-ed* ending examples.**

Questions and short answers

To make questions in the past, we use *did*.
To make short positive answers, we also use *did*.
To make negative answers and sentences, we use *didn't*.
Examples **A** Did he stay there? **B** Yes, he did.
  A Did you check in? **B** No, I didn't.

Wh- questions

To make *Wh-* questions, we use *did*.
Example **A** What did Waldorf Astor do?
  B He built the Waldorf-Astoria Hotel.

be in the Past Simple

Positive
It **was** the first luxury hotel.
The lifts **were** electric.

We use *was* for *I*, *he*, *she*, and *it* (single things).
We use *were* for *you*, *we*, and *they* (two or more people or things).

Use

We use the Past Simple to talk about actions or situations in the past.
Examples The hotel opened in 1889.
Marilyn Monroe lived in the hotel for several months.

PRACTICE **1 Write these sentences in the Past Simple.**

1 It's a luxury hotel. _____
2 She is a celebrity. _____
3 There are four lifts. _____
4 The guests are famous. _____
5 He lives in Jamaica. _____
6 It closes in 2010. _____

2 ◆) **8.11 Listen and complete the table with these words.**

danced started painted lived stayed filmed
opened worked finished played invented moved

/d/	/t/	/ɪd/

3 **Complete the answers.**

1 Did the Beatles stay at the Savoy Hotel? Yes, _____ _____.
2 Did Monet paint in the Waldorf Hotel? No, _____ _____.
3 Did Frank Sinatra play the piano? Yes, _____ _____.
4 Did Marilyn Monroe live in the Waldorf Hotel? Yes, _____ _____.
5 Did Elizabeth Taylor dance on the roof of the Savoy Hotel? No, _____
_____.

4 **Read about Raffles Hotel. Complete the answers.**

Raffles Hotel in Singapore opened in 1887. It was a small hotel with ten bedrooms at first. Syed Abdul Rahman Alsagoff developed the hotel and added electric lights and fans. Many famous people stayed there. Charlie Chaplin was a guest at the hotel in 1933. Many famous writers and film stars stayed at the hotel, for example, John Wayne, Ava Gardner, Ernest Hemingway, and Joseph Conrad. The barman, Ngiam Tong Boom, created the famous cocktail, the Singapore Sling. The owners, Fairmont Raffles Hotel International, started upgrading the hotel in 1989. The hotel opened again two years later.

1 When did the hotel open? It _____ in 1887.
2 What did Syed Abdul Rahman Alsagoff do? He _____ the hotel and _____ electric lights and fans.
3 What did Ngiam Tong Boom do? He _____ the famous cocktail, the Singapore Sling.
4 When did Charlie Chaplin stay at the hotel? He _____ at the hotel in 1933.
5 What did the owners do in 1989? They _____ upgrading the hotel.

Vocabulary Hotels

1 **Match the verbs with the nouns.**

Verbs		Nouns
1 make a	a	credit card
2 go to	b	passport
3 carry your	c	reservation
4 pay by	d	bags
5 fill in the	e	reception
6 show your	f	lift
7 take the	g	registration form

2 Match these things with the actions 1–6.

television   *bed*   *wardrobe*   *window*   *light*
bathroom   *bath*   *shower*   *towel*   *door*

1 You sleep on it.   _____
2 You wash here.   _____
3 You open or close it.   _____
4 You turn it on or off.   _____
5 You watch it.   _____
6 You dry yourself with it. _____

3 What are the mystery objects?

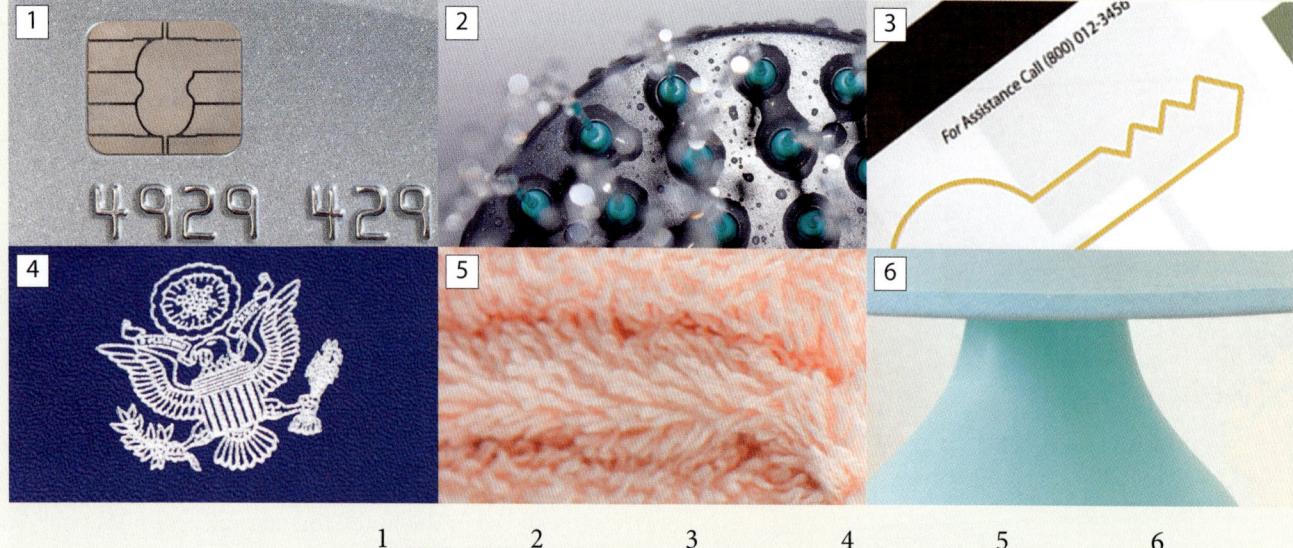

1 _____   2 _____   3 _____   4 _____   5 _____   6 _____

Work skills Giving and checking information

Complete the telephone conversation.

A Hello. I'd like to make a reservation.

B Certainly. Could I have your _____[1], please?

A Richard Deccard.

B I'm sorry. Could you _____[2] that, please?

A _____ _____[3].

B Is that with two _____[4]s?

A Yes, that's right. I'd like to book a room from Friday 30th September for two nights.

B Let me just check. Is that from Friday 30th September to _____ _____[5]?

A That's correct.

B Would you like a single or double room?

A _____ _____[6] is a double room?

B A double room is 240 euros per night.

A That's fine.

B Let me just check availability. OK. So your booking is for _____[7] nights from _____[8] to _____[9] for a _____[10] room at _____[11] euros per night. Your confirmation number is 89637.

A I'm sorry, it's a bit noisy. Could you _____ _____[12] again, please?

B Yes, your confirmation number is 89637.

A Thank you very much.

B Thank you. Goodbye.

A Goodbye.

Functions Checking in and out of a hotel

We use the following expressions when we check in and out.

	Guest	**Hotel staff**
Check-in	I'd like to check in, please.	Could you fill in the registration form, please?
	Is there a lift?	Here's your key card.
		Have you got any bags?
		You are in room 306.
		Do you have your passport and credit card?
Check-out	I'd like to check out, please.	Have you got your key card?
		Here's your bill.
		How would you like to pay?

PRACTICE

1 Complete the conversation.

A Good afternoon, madam.

B Hello. My name's Hanisch. I'd like to _____¹, please.

A OK. Could you _____² your name, please?

B H-A-N-I-S-C-H. Hanisch.

A Ah yes, here we are. A single room for five _____³.

B Yes, that's right.

A Could you _____⁴ in the registration form, please?

B Of course.

A And could I see your _____⁵ and _____⁶?

B Yes, here you are.

A Thank you. Here's your _____⁷ card, Ms Hanisch. You _____⁸ in room 475. That's on the fourth _____⁹.

B Is there a lift?

A Yes, it's next to the main door. Have you got any _____¹⁰?

B Yes, I have three suitcases.

A Would you like the _____¹¹ to take them to your room?

B Yes, please.

A No problem.

B Thank you.

2 Order the conversation.

A Good morning. I'd like to check out, please. Room 222.	*1*
B How would you like to pay?	___
B Thank you. Room 222 … One moment please, sir. … Here's your bill. Would you like to check it?	___
A Yes, here it is.	___
B Of course. No problem. Have you got your key card, sir?	___
B Thank you. Here's your receipt. Have a nice day. Goodbye.	___
A Yes, please. … It's fine.	___
A Goodbye.	___
A Cash.	___

All around the world

Grammar Past Simple: irregular verbs; questions with *be*

INTRODUCTION   **1**   Read about an amazing journey. Answer the questions.

Amazing Journey

In 2010, Vin Cox went round the world on a bicycle. He travelled 18,000 miles through 17 countries. It took 163 days.

He came back to England on 1st August.

The journey began in England in February 2010.

The weather in Dakota in the USA wasn't good.

He went to France. It was very cold, −7°C.

In North Africa the temperature rose to 50°C.

He got very sick in Libya.

Cycling was very dangerous in Rajasthan, India.

He met his friends in Brisbane, Australia.

He didn't visit Antarctica because it doesn't have any roads.

1 When did Vin begin his journey?   _____
2 Where did he go first?   _____
3 Was France cold?   _____
4 What happened in Libya?   _____
5 What did he do in Australia?   _____
6 Was the weather good in the USA?   _____
7 Did he visit Antarctica? Why / Why not? _____
8 When did he come back to England?   _____

Focus

Read the examples.

The journey **began** in England in February 2010.
He **got** sick in Libya.
He **met** his friends in Brisbane.

To make the Past Simple for irregular verbs, we use a different form of the verb.
See the list in the Review.

Read the examples.

Was France cold?
The weather in Dakota in the USA **wasn't** good.

Complete the rules.

To form a question in the Past Simple with *be*, we use *Was/Were* + _____ + adjective.
To form the negative in the Past Simple with *be*, we use _____ and *weren't*.

▶ For more details and practice, go to the Review section on pages 92 and 93.

PRACTICE   **2** ●)) **9.1 Listen to the second part of Vin's story. Complete the answers.**

1 How did he make breakfast?
   He _____ his breakfast with a small gas stove.
2 Where did he eat lunch?
   He _____ some of his meals in cafés and motels.
3 Where did he sleep?
   He _____ in a very small tent.
4 What did he take with him?
   He _____ two mobile phones, two video cameras, a cup and spoon, a sleeping bag.
5 Did he take any clothes?
   Yes, he _____ a shirt, shorts, and pants.
6 What sort of bike did he ride?
   He _____ a Genesis racing bike.
7 What did he see and do?
   He _____ lots of beautiful scenery and _____ a lot of experiences, some good, some bad.
8 Was it dangerous?
   Sometimes. Cycling _____ very dangerous in Rajasthan in India.
9 Why did he do it?
   He _____ it to make money for a charity.
10 How much did he make?
   He _____ about £18,000.

3 Write the Past Simple form of these verbs from *Amazing Journey*.

Irregular verb	Past Simple	Irregular verb	Past Simple
go	_____ 1	take	_____ 6
have	_____ 2	begin	_____ 7
get	_____ 3	rise	_____ 8
make	_____ 4	sleep	_____ 9
eat	_____ 5	come	_____ 10

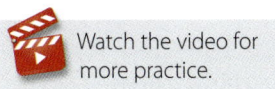
Watch the video for more practice.

4 Work in pairs. Ask and answer the questions in 2.

TASK   **5 Work in pairs. Ask and answer questions about a trip you made.**

Where did you go?	What did you see?	What did you take with you?
How did you travel?	What did you eat?	Who did you meet?
What did you do?	Where did you sleep?	Was it fun?

Vocabulary Locations

1 **Find these things on the map of the town centre.**

1 a place to have lunch   _restaurant_
2 a place to buy stamps   _____
3 a place to buy a shirt   _____
4 a place to catch a train   _____
5 a place to watch a film   _____

6 a place to see old things and paintings   _____
7 a place to have a coffee   _____
8 a place to get money   _____

2 **Find these things on the map.**

1 the pavement   _c_
2 the road   ___
3 a corner   ___
4 the end of Ocean Road   ___
5 traffic lights   ___

3 ◗)) **9.2 Marta is asking a friend about the town. Listen and write the places on the map.**

A Where is the library?
B It's on Ocean Road, between the bank and the post office.
A Is there a bookshop in town?
B Yes. It's on Park Road, opposite the cinema.
A Where's the hotel?
B It's at the end of Ocean Road, next to the restaurant.
A Is there a supermarket?
B Yes. It's on the corner of Ocean Road and Park Road, opposite the post office.

4 **Look at the map. Complete the sentences.**

1 A Where's the post office?
   B It's on _____ Road, _____ the library and the clothes shop.
2 A Is there a cinema in town?
   B Yes. It's on _____ Road, _____ to the café.
3 A Where's the museum?
   B It's on the _____ of Ocean Road and _____ Road, _____ the department store.

5 **Work in pairs. Ask and answer about places on the map.**

Work skills Looking after a visitor

1 **Complete Pat Dawson's part of the conversation with the sentences a–h.**

A Good morning. I'm Ajeet Singh from Tata Motors. I have a meeting with Ms Jensen.

B _____
_____ 1

A Nice to meet you too, Pat.

B _____ 2

A It was quite long, about 12 hours. But the service was very good.

B _____ 3

A It's near your office, and it's very comfortable.

B _____
_____ 4

A Yes, I'll have a coffee, please.

B _____ 5

A Just milk, please.

B _____ 6

A OK. I have a copy with me.

B _____ 7

A That's right. Three o'clock. Is the meeting in this office?

B _____ 8

A No, I don't think so.

B OK. Please come this way.

A Thank you very much. It's my first time here …

a No problem. With milk and sugar?
b Good morning, Mr Singh. I'm Pat Dawson, Ms Jensen's PA. Nice to meet you.
c No, it's in the main meeting room. Can I help you with anything else?
d Good. And how is the hotel?
e OK. … So, shall we go through your schedule …?
f That's great. Your meeting with Ms Jensen is at three o'clock.
g How was your flight?
h Excellent. Would you like a drink?

2 ◉)) **9.3** **Listen and check your answers.**

3 **Answer these questions about the conversation in 1.**

1 Who does Ajeet Singh work for? _____
2 How was his flight? _____
3 Where is the hotel? _____
4 Does he want a drink? _____
5 Does he have his schedule with him? _____
6 Where is the meeting? _____

4 **Work in pairs. Practise the conversation in 1.**

5 **Practise the conversation again.**

Student A Use your own name and company. Your meeting is with Mr Martin at 11.30.

Student B You work for Mr Martin. The meeting is in the conference room at 11.30.

Functions Asking for and giving directions

1 **Match the sentences 1–7 with the pictures a–g.**

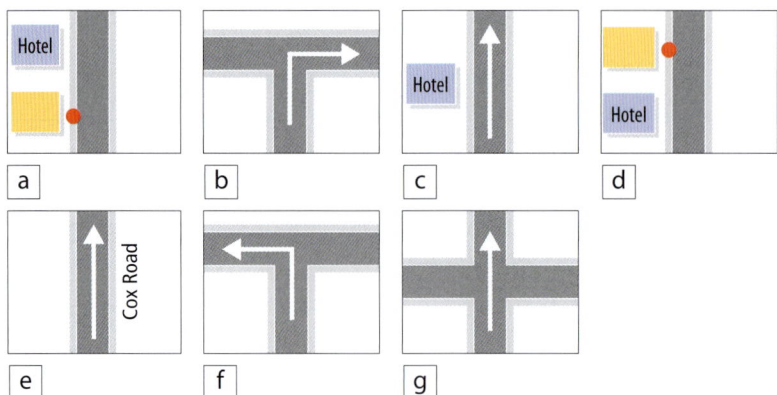

1 Go down Cox Road. _e_
2 Turn left. ___
3 Go straight on. ___
4 Turn right. ___

5 It's on the left, before the hotel. ___
6 It's on the left, after the hotel. ___
7 Go past the hotel. ___

2 •)) 9.4 **Look at the map. Listen to three conversations. The people are at the bus stop. Circle the places they want to go to.**

1 A Excuse me. Where is the …?
   B It's on Park Street. Go straight on, past Station Hill Road. Then turn right at the coffee shop into Park Street. It's on the left, next to the chemist.
   A Thank you.

2 A Excuse me. How do I get to the …?
   B Go down this road to the end. Turn left and it's on the right, just before the sports centre.
   A Thank you.

3 A Hi. Is there a … near here?
   B Yes, there is. Go down Queen's Road. Then turn left at the cinema into Station Hill Road. It's at the end on the right.
   A Thank you.

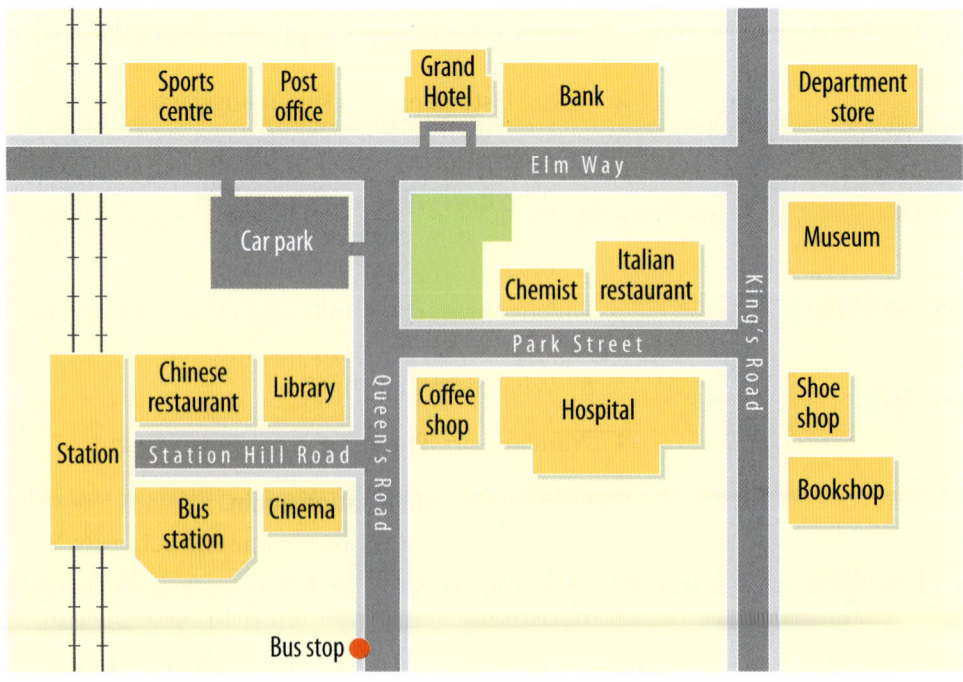

PRACTICE

3 Look at the map in **2**. Complete the conversations. You are at the bus stop.

1 A Hi. Is there a bookshop near here?
   B Yes, there's one on King's Road. Go _____¹ this road.
   A OK.
   B Turn _____² at the coffee shop. Go to the end of _____ _____³.
      Turn right into King's Road. The bookshop is on the _____⁴, after the
      _____⁵ shop.
   A Thanks very much.

2 A Excuse me. How do I get to the department store?
   B Go down this road to the _____¹. Turn right.
   A OK.
   B Go _____² Elm Way, _____³ the bank, and King's Road. The
      department store is on the _____⁴.

3 A Excuse me. Where is the bus station?
   B It's on Station Hill Road. Go down this road. Turn _____¹ at the
      cinema. Go to the _____² of the road and it's on your _____³.
   A Thank you.

TASK

4 Work in pairs. Student A, go to page 107. Student B, go to page 109. Give your
partner directions to places on the map.

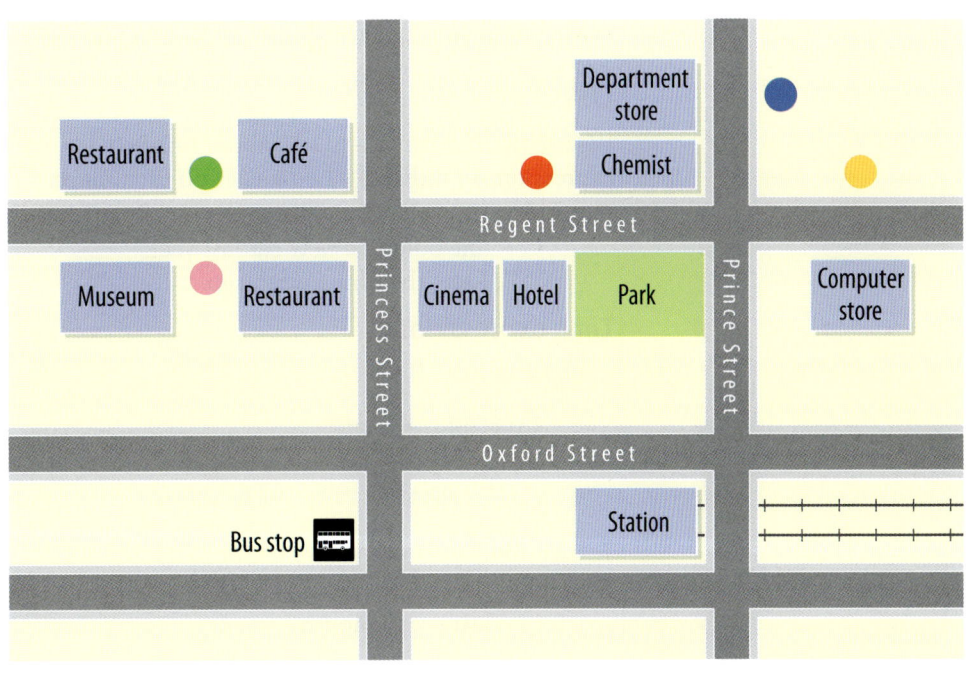

Review

Grammar Past Simple: irregular verbs; questions with *be*

Form

To form many verbs in the Past Simple, we use *-ed* (see unit 8). Irregular verbs have a different form. There is a longer list of common irregular verbs in the Pocket Book.

Infinitive	Past Simple	Infinitive	Past Simple
go	went	get	got
come	came	make	made
meet	met	eat	ate
see	saw	begin	began
buy	bought	rise	rose
have	had	sleep	slept

There are some patterns to help you learn some irregular past tenses.
For example:

1 Change the vowel sound in the verb to /ɔː/ (sounds like *door*).
Examples buy bought   catch caught   teach taught   think thought

2 Change the vowel sound in the verb to /əʊ/ (sounds like *no*).
Examples choose chose   speak spoke

3 Some verbs do not change at all. They are the same in the Present Simple and in the Past Simple:
Examples cut cut   cost cost   put put

The Past Simple form is the same for all persons: *I went, you went, he went*, etc.
We use *did* + verb to make questions and negatives.
Examples When did Vin begin his journey?
        He didn't have space for more clothes.

To make questions with *be*, we use *was/were*, the subject, and an adjective.
Examples Was it cold in India?
        Were the people in Indonesia friendly?

We form the negative with *was not / wasn't* and *were not / weren't*.

Use

We use the Past Simple to talk about finished actions in the past. We can use time expressions to indicate when an action took place.
Examples I went to Guangdong in 2009.
        She bought a new car last year.
        I saw the film a week ago.

Time expressions

Look at the time line.

a year ago / last year

2013   NOW / 2014

To talk about past events, we use *ago* and *last*.
Examples two years / months / weeks ago
        last year / month / week

PRACTICE

1 Choose the correct verb.

1 Last year, he *buy / bought* his first sports car.
2 When did he *come / came* to Japan?
3 *Was / Were* cycling in India dangerous?
4 We didn't *sell / sold* many units.
5 Yesterday, I *speak / spoke* to Claude.
6 Did you *win / won* the prize?
7 Why did they *have / had* a meeting on Wednesday?
8 They didn't *buy / bought* the yacht.
9 Where *is / was* the conference last year?
10 *Was / Were* the weather in North Africa good?

2 Tick ✓ the things you did last week.

Last week, did you …?
buy a newspaper ☐
go on a business trip ☐
speak to your boss ☐
go to a restaurant ☐
see an old friend ☐
begin a new project ☐

3 Write sentences about the things you did or didn't do last week. Use the information in 2.

_____
_____
_____
_____
_____
_____

Vocabulary Locations

1 Match the words 1–5 with the pictures a–e.

1 between   ___
2 opposite   ___
3 at the end of ___
4 next to   ___
5 on the corner of ___

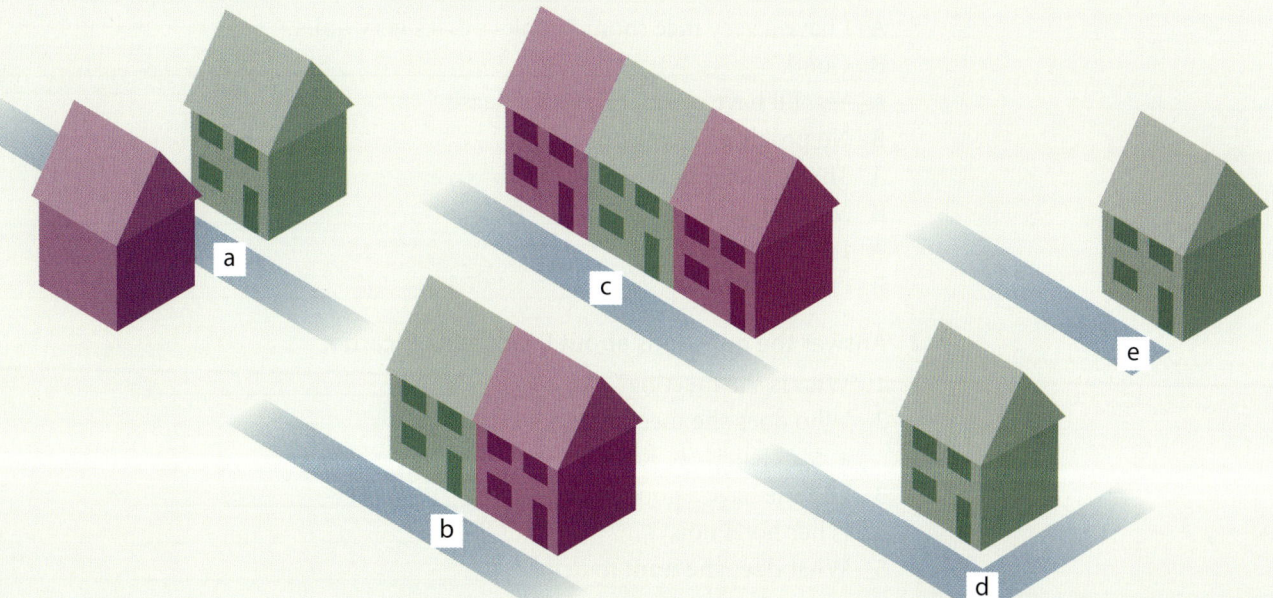

2 Look at the two pictures. Find five differences. Then write sentences to say what is different. Use *next to, between, opposite*.

Example   In picture A, there is a man next to the car.
In picture B, a woman is next to the car.

Work skills Looking after a visitor

1 Complete the conversation. Use these phrases.

Can I help you with anything else?   *Please come this way.*   *How is the hotel?*
How was your flight this morning?   *Would you like a drink?*   *Pleased to meet you.*

A Good afternoon. I'm Evangelina Ricardo. I have a meeting with Mr Henri.

B Good afternoon, Ms Ricardo. I'm Kevin. I'm Mr Henri's assistant.

_____ 1

A Pleased to meet you too.

B _____ 2

A It was fine, thank you.

B _____ 3

A I have a very nice room, thank you. It's very quiet.

B Good. _____ 4

A Yes, I'll have a mineral water, please.

B No problem. Here you are.

A Thank you very much.

B My pleasure. _____ 5

A I don't think so.

B OK. _____ 6

2 Answer the questions about Evangelina Ricardo.

1   Who is she meeting?   _____

2   Who does she meet first?
    a Mr Henri   b Kevin   _____

3   Did she have a good flight? _____

4   Is her hotel noisy?   _____

5   What does she want to drink? _____

Functions Asking for and giving directions

Asking for directions

We use these questions to ask the way to a place.

Examples Where is the bank?
Is there a coffee shop near here?
How do I get to the hospital?

We usually say *Excuse me* first and *Thank you* at the end.

Giving directions

To say where a place is, we use prepositions of location.

Examples It's on Bolivar Road.
It's next to the bus station.
It's opposite the supermarket.
It's on the left.
It's between the station and the cinema.

To give directions, we use the verb. The verb form doesn't change.

Examples Go straight on.
Turn left at the hotel.
Turn right onto Green Street.

PRACTICE

1 **Match the questions 1–3 with the answers a–c.**

1 Where's the hospital?
2 Is there a cinema near here?
3 How do I get to the chemist?

a No, there isn't. Sorry.
b Turn left at the hotel. It's next to the coffee shop.
c It's opposite the park.

2 **Look at the map. You are in the New Hotel on Elgar Road. Complete the conversation.**

A _____¹ me. _____² the station?
B It's on _____ _____³.
A _____⁴ do I get there?
B Go out of the hotel and _____⁵ right. Go straight on. Then _____ _____⁶ into Queen's Road. The station is on the _____⁷, _____⁸ the park.
A Thank you very much.
B No problem.

10 Making plans

Grammar *going to*

1 ◉) **10.1 Kay Hudson is preparing for a business trip. Listen and complete the sentences with the correct verbs.**

get   ask   learn   fly   meet   send   book   call   arrange   email   invite   buy

This morning, I'm going to _____ [1] my flight, a return flight from London to Hong Kong. I'm going to _____ [2] Cathay Pacific this time. People say the food and service are really good. Then I'm going to _____ [3] Yiyi Chen in Hong Kong. She's going to _____ [4] me at Chek Lap Kok Airport, so I'm going to _____ [5] her the flight details.

Tomorrow morning, I'm going to _____ [6] Joseph Nolan in Hong Kong to talk about my trip. He's going to _____ [7] a meeting with our new partners, DesignHK. They are a design company who are going to design some of our new products. I'm going to _____ [8] everyone from DesignHK for a nice dinner. The restaurant I went to last year was terrible so I'm going to _____ [9] Joseph for some suggestions.

I'm going to _____ [10] some Hong Kong dollars from the bank. I've got a credit card but cash is really useful for taxis and snacks and things. I'm going to _____ [11] some new summer clothes because it's going to be hot in Hong Kong. And finally, my Chinese is really bad, so I'm going to _____ [12] ten new phrases and practise them on the journey.

2 Answer the questions about Kay's trip.

1 Where is Kay going to fly to? _____
2 What's Yiyi going to do? _____
3 What's Joseph going to do? _____
4 What are DesignHK going to do? _____
5 Who is Kay going to invite for dinner? _____

PRACTICE

3 **Make sentences about things Kay Hudson is going to do.**

Example   She's going to fly to Hong Kong.

1 book / flight / Hong Kong
2 send / Yiyi Chen / flight details
3 call / Joseph Nolan
4 ask / him / suggestions about restaurants
5 get / Hong Kong dollars / bank
6 buy / summer clothes
7 learn / ten new phrases in Chinese

4 **Complete the sentences about Kay Hudson's trip with these verbs.**

are   fly   are   do   am   visit   have   meet   stay   go   we are

Next week, I _____¹ going to visit our partners, DesignHK in Hong Kong. Joseph and I _____² going to _____³ the DesignHK team on Tuesday and then we _____⁴ going to _____⁵ their factory on Wednesday.

I'm going to _____⁶ at the Peninsula Hotel. I'm free on Thursday, so I'm going to _____⁷ some shopping and then I'm going to _____⁸ sightseeing in Kowloon. In the evening, I'm going to meet my old friend, Doctor Wu, and _____⁹ going to _____¹⁰ dinner at the hotel. I'm going to _____¹¹ back to London on Friday.

TASK

5 **You are going to go on a sports holiday. Choose the type of holiday.**

Sport	skiing	diving	mountain climbing
Place	Himalayas	Swiss Alps	Maldive Islands
	Hawaii	Thailand	Rocky Mountains
Place to stay	hotel	tent	boat
Things to take	skis	wet suit	climbing boots
	ski jacket	towel	sweater
	map	mask	
Time	next week	in the winter/summer holidays	
	next year	in January/July	
How long	one week	two weeks	a month

6 **Work in pairs. Tell your partner about your plans.**

Example   I'm going to go diving. I'm going to take …

Vocabulary Countries, nationalities, and brands

1 Match the brands 1–10 with the pictures a–j.

1 Gucci	___	5 Ikea	___	9 Rolex	___
2 Vodafone	___	6 Perrier	___	10 Adidas	___
3 McDonald's	___	7 Apple	___		
4 Zara	___	8 Toyota	___		

2 ◗) **10.2** Listen. Write the nationality for the countries.

	Country	Nationality		Country	Nationality
1	Spain	_____	6	Italy	_____
2	Germany	_____	7	the USA	_____
3	Sweden	_____	8	France	_____
4	Japan	_____	9	Britain	_____
5	South Korea	_____	10	Switzerland	_____

3 Make sentences about the companies in **1**.

Example   Gucci is an Italian company. It makes bags.

4 ◗) **10.3** Listen and check your answers.

5 Work in pairs. Match the airlines with the nationalities. Student A, go to page 107. Student B, go to page 109. Check your answers.

Example   **Student A** Is Cathay Pacific a Russian airline?
              Student B No, it isn't. It's …

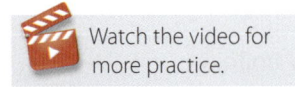
Watch the video for more practice.

6 ◗) **10.4** Listen and repeat.

Work skills Emails 3

1 Read the email.

To:	Kay Hudson
From:	Joseph Nolan
Subject:	DesignHK
Date:	12.07.14
Attachment:	📄 Design 1 📄 Design 2

Hi Kay,

I met Cham Li and Jenny Chan from DesignHK yesterday.
I've got some bad news. They asked for an extra 10%. The price we agreed was $100,000.
I'm OK with 5%. What do you think?
Also they want two months. I really want the new design next month. Is September OK?
The good news is the first designs are really great. Two PDF files attached. Do you like them?
I'm going to meet Cham and Jenny for lunch. Can you call me before 12.00?
Speak to you soon,
Joseph

2 Answer the questions.

1 What is the bad news? _____
2 Does Joseph think $105,000 is OK? _____
3 Does Joseph think September is OK? _____
4 What does Joseph think of the designs? _____

3 Match Joseph's phrases 1–5 with the descriptions a–c.

1 The good news is …   a introduce bad news _____
2 What do you think?   b introduce good news _____
3 I've got some bad news.   c ask for Kay's opinion _____
4 Is September OK?
5 Do you like them?

4 Read Kay's reply.

To:	Joseph Nolan
From:	Kay Hudson
Subject:	DesignHK problem
Date:	12.07.14

Hi Joseph,

I'm pleased you met Cham and Jenny yesterday. I'm sorry to hear about the extra 10%. Do you mean DesignHK want $110,000? I think this is too much. I agree with you. $105,000 is OK. It's great about the designs. I like them a lot.
I'll call you at 11.00.

Thanks for all your help,
Kay

5 Match Kay's phrases 1–5 with the descriptions a–d.

1 I think …   a respond to good news _____
2 I'm pleased …   b respond to bad news _____
3 Do you mean …?   c give her opinion _____
4 I'm sorry to hear about …   d check a question _____
5 It's great about …

Functions Saying *thank you* and *goodbye*

INTRODUCTION   **1** •)) **10.5** Listen and read the conversations.

1 **Kay** Bye, Joseph. And thanks for everything.
   Joseph You're welcome! I'll be in touch again about the DesignHK project.
   Kay Great.
   Joseph Have a good flight.
   Kay Thanks. Bye!

3 **Antonia** Bye, Maia. It was lovely to meet you.
   Maia Yes, it was great working together.
   Antonia I look forward to working with you again.
   Maia Me too. Bye, Antonia.

2 **Claudia** Goodbye, Mario. It was nice to see you again. I hope you have a safe journey home.
   Mario Thank you.
   Claudia See you again next month.
   Mario I look forward to it. Goodbye.
   Claudia Goodbye.

4 **Claire** Thank you very much for coming. Your presentation was very interesting.
   Ian My pleasure.
   Claire I'll call you next week.
   Ian Thank you. Bye for now.
   Claire Bye.

2 Complete the sentences about the people in **1**.

1 _____ is going to work with _____ again.
2 _____ is going to call _____ next week.
3 _____ and _____ are going to meet next month.
4 _____ is going to contact _____ about the DesignHK project.

Focus

Complete the table with these phrases.

Thank you very much for coming.   *It was lovely to meet you.*
I'll be in touch again.   *Bye.*
Have a good flight.   *I look forward to it / working with you again.*
Thanks for everything.   *Goodbye.*
It was nice to see you again.   *See you again next month.*
I'll call you next week.   *I hope you have a safe journey.*
It was great working together.   *Bye for now.*

Thanking someone	
Wishing someone a good trip home	
Saying you enjoyed meeting	
Talking about future contact	
Saying goodbye	

▶ For more details and practice, go to the Review section on page 105.

PRACTICE

3 Order the conversations.

1 a I look forward to it. Bye for now. ___
  b Bye, James. It was really lovely to meet you. I hope you have a safe journey home. ___
  c Bye. ___
  d Thanks, Rebecca. See you again next month. ___

2 a My pleasure. It was great working together. ___
  b Bye for now. ___
  c I'll be in touch again soon. ___
  d It was nice to see you again, Lynn. Thanks for everything. ___
  e Bye, Greg. ___
  f Great. ___

3 a Great. Goodbye. ___
  b My pleasure. I look forward to working with you again, Helen. ___
  c Goodbye. ___
  d Thank you very much for coming, Paul. It was a very useful meeting. ___
  e I'll be in touch next week. ___

TASK

4 Say *thank you* and *goodbye* to people in the class.

Example   Bye, Hamid. Thanks for everything.
        Bye, Patricia. See you again next year.

Review

Grammar *going to*

Form

We form the *going to* future with *be* + *going to* + verb.
Example   Kay is going to contact Joseph.

We can use the short form of *be*.
Examples I'm going to have a haircut.
                    She's going to invite them for dinner.

Use

We use *going to* to talk about intentions and plans for the future.
Example   Antonia and Maia are going to work together again.

PRACTICE   **1** **Complete the sentences and correct the information.**

1 Kay *is*_____ going to fly to ~~Thailand.~~ *Hong Kong*
2 She's going to _____ British Airways.
3 Yiyi and Kay _____ going to meet at the hotel.
4 Joseph's going to invite everyone from DesignHK for _____.
5 Kay and Doctor Wu _____ going to have lunch together.
6 Kay is going to _____ some new shoes.
7 She _____ going to get some money at the airport.
8 She's going to _____ five phrases in Japanese.

2 **You are going to have an interview for a new job. Match the sentences 1–7 with the ideas a–g.**

1 Your suit is really old.   ___
2 You don't know about the company. ___
3 You don't know how to get there.   ___
4 Your hair is too long.   ___
5 Your CV is out of date.   ___
6 Your presentation isn't ready.   ___
7 You are not good at interviews.   ___

a have a haircut
b check the map
c practise the interview with a friend
d finish my presentation
e buy a new suit
f look at the company website
g write a new CV

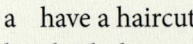

3 **Write what you are going to do before the interview.**

Example   I'm going to have a haircut.

Vocabulary Countries, nationalities, and brands

1 Label the flags with the nationalities. Use these words.

Chinese   British   French   American   Italian   Dutch
Japanese   Saudi Arabian   Argentinian   Brazilian   Spanish   Russian

1 _____   2 _____   3 _____   4 _____   5 _____   6 _____

7 _____   8 _____   9 _____   10 _____   11 _____   12 _____

2 Write about five things you've got or like.

Examples   I've got a Prada bag. It's Italian.
            I like sushi. It's Japanese.

_____
_____
_____
_____
_____

3 Complete the table for these airlines.

Airline	Country	Nationality
1 Virgin Airlines	Britain	_____
2 Delta	_____	American
3 JAL	Japan	_____
4 Lufthansa	_____	German
5 Qantas	Australia	_____
6 Thai Airways	_____	Thai

4 Make sentences about the airlines.

Example   Virgin Airlines is a British company.

_____
_____
_____
_____
_____

5 Find these countries from the unit on the map.

Thailand
Spain
South Korea
Germany
Sweden
Japan
Italy
the USA
Argentina

France
Britain
Australia
China
Holland
Saudi Arabia
Switzerland
Brazil
Russia

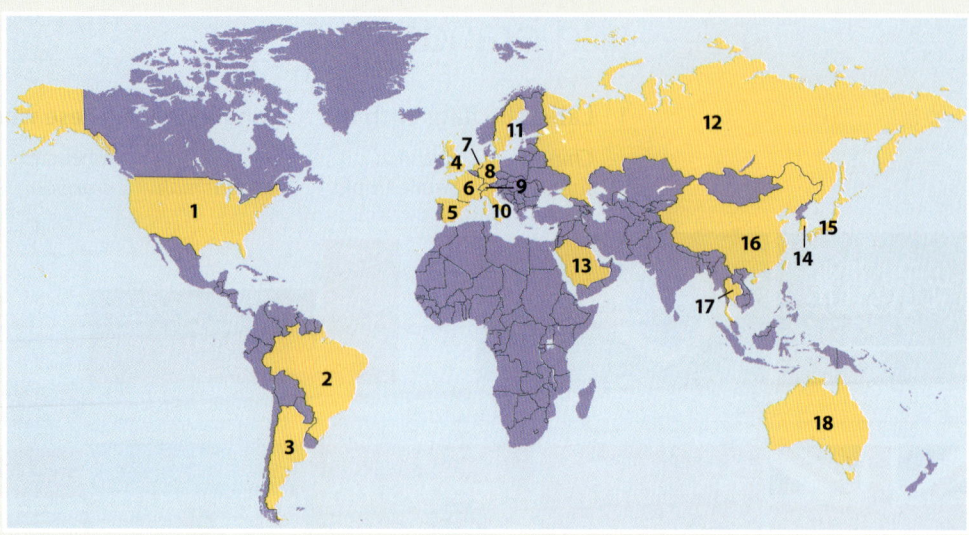

Work skills Emails 3

1 Complete Joseph's email with these words.

think   attached   call   I've got   like   good news

From: Joseph Nolan
To: Kay Hudson
Subject: DesignHK
Sent: 12.07.14
Attachment: 📄 New design 1 📄 New design 2 📄 New design 3 📄 New design 4 📄 New design 5

Hi Kay,

_____¹ some bad news. DesignHK now want another $50,000. They say the design was very difficult and it took a long time. What do you _____²?
The _____³ is that the designs are finished. Five PDF files _____⁴. Do you _____⁵ them?
I'm going to meet Cham and Jenny tomorrow. Can you _____⁶ me today?

Speak to you soon,
Joseph

2 Complete Kay's email with these words.

I think   call   sorry to hear   pleased   Do you mean

From: Kay Hudson
To: Joseph Nolan
Subject: DesignHK problem
Sent: 12.07.14

Hi Joseph,

I'm _____¹ about the extra $50.000. _____² DesignHK want $150,000? _____³ this is too much.
I'm _____⁴ about the designs. They all look really good.
I'll _____⁵ you this afternoon.

Regards,
Kay

Functions Saying *thankyou* and *goodbye*

After a business trip, it is polite to say *thank you* and *goodbye*.

Examples   Thanks for everything.
               Thanks for all your help.
               Goodbye!

We can wish someone a good trip home.

Examples   Have a good flight.
               I hope you have a safe journey.

We can say that we enjoyed the meeting.

Examples   It was really lovely to meet you.
               It was great working together.

We can talk about future plans.

Examples   See you again next month.
               I'll be in touch soon.
               Until next time.

PRACTICE

1 Order the conversation.

Ms Oxendon	I will. See you next summer!	___
Ms Sasaki	Please say thank you to Karl from me.	___
Ms Oxendon	Goodbye.	___
Ms Oxendon	You're welcome.	___
Ms Sasaki	Thank you. And thank you for everything.	___
Ms Sasaki	Goodbye.	___
Ms Oxendon	Goodbye, Shiho. I hope you have a safe journey home.	___

2 ◉)) **10. 6 Listen and check your answers.**

3 Choose the best responses.

1 It was great to meet you.
  a You too.   b Until next time.

2 Thank you for everything.
  a I hope you have a safe journey.
  b You're welcome.

3 Have a good flight.
  a Goodbye.   b Thanks.

4 It was great working with you.
  a It was lovely to meet you too.
  b You too.

Task and activity notes

1 Work skills p.9

Student A. Introduce yourself and spell these names for Student B.

1   Ajeet Singh
2   Lauren Nzunga
3   Lisa Chang

7 Grammar p.67

Complete the questions. Answer them for yourself. Then ask three people in the class. Complete the table.

	You	1	2	3
Company (Which …?)				
Job (What …?)				
Location (Where …?)				
People (Who …?)				

7 Work skills p.69

Student A

You are Momoko. Write to Andrea.

1   Tell her about a change in the dates.
    Outbound   Wednesday 18 November
    Inbound   Thursday 26 November
2   Ask her the name of her hotel in Tokyo.

8 Grammar p.77

Student A

Hotel Quiz

Ask your partner these questions. They get one point for a correct answer and one for a correct sentence using the Past Simple.

1   Which hotel did Elizabeth Taylor love?
2   Which famous salad did the Waldorf-Astoria chef create?
3   Did Marilyn Monroe live in the Savoy Hotel?
4   What did Fred Astaire do at the Savoy Hotel?
5   Did George Boldt build the Waldorf-Astoria?

9 **Functions** p.91

Student A

1 Give directions to the bank.

We are at the bus stop. Go down Princess Street. Turn right at the cinema. Go past the hotel. Turn left at the chemist. The bank is opposite the department store.

2 Ask for directions to the bookshop. Which colour circle is it?

10 **Vocabulary** p.98

Student A

Match the airlines and the nationalities. Check your answers with Student B.

Spanish   British   Italian   Russian   Chinese

1	LOT	Polish
2	Cathay Pacific	
3	Delta	American
4	EasyJet	
5	All Nippon Airways	Japanese
6	Aeroflot	
7	TAM	Brazilian
8	Iberia	
9	KLM	Dutch
10	Alitalia	

Example   **Student A** Is Cathay Pacific a Russian airline?
                  Student B No, it isn't. It's …

6 **Functions** p.61

Work in groups of three. Read the menu and order a meal.

Waiter	A	B
Are you ready to order?	Yes, I'd like …	And I'll have …
	Do you have any …?	Can we have some …?
And what would you like to drink?	I'll have …	And I'd like …
Thank you.		

La Trattoria

Starters

Garlic bread   Bruschetta
    Soup   Ham & melon

Fish

Salmon   Sea bass
Red snapper   Fried squid &
                              prawns

Pasta

Spaghetti   Cannelloni
Rigatoni   Lasagne
Tagliatelle   Gnocchi

Pizza

Margherita   Calabrese
    Funghi   Sicilian
        Capri   Vegetarian

La Trattoria

Side dishes

Green beans   Polenta
    Zucchini   Focaccia

Salad

Spinach salad   Caesar salad
Italian salad   Caprino salad

Desserts

Cheesecake   Tiramisu
    Canoli   Torte
    Biscotti   Gelato

Drinks

    Tea
                         Orange juice
Cappucino   Mineral water
Espresso   Red / white wine

1   Work skills p.9

Student B. Introduce yourself and spell these names for Student A.

1   Charlotte Charlesworth
2   Daisuke Nakamoto
3   Klaus Schmitt

7   Work skills p.69

Student B

You are Andrea. You have new information from Momoko.

1   There is a change in dates.

     Outbound   Wednesday 18 November
     Inbound   Thursday 26 November

2   Your hotel is the Park Hyatt, Shinjuku,

     Email Momoko. Say the new dates are OK. Tell her the name of the hotel.

8   Work skills p.79

Student B

You are the hotel receptionist. Listen to Student A. Change the details on the registration form.

Guest name	Jenny Ostin	Departure date	7th March
Confirmation number	552739	Room type	Single
Arrival date	5th March	Room rate per night	216 euros

Example   **You**   Could I have your name, please?
               Student A   Yes, it's …

8   Grammar p.77

Student B

Hotel Quiz

Ask your partner these questions. They get one point for a correct answer and one for a correct sentence using the Past Simple.

1 Did Monet paint pictures from the Savoy Hotel?
2 What sort of salad dressing did George Boldt introduce?
3 Who played piano in the American Bar at the Savoy?
4 Which hotel did Princess Grace of Monaco stay in?
5 Did the Savoy Hotel open in 1889 or 1989?

9   Functions p.91

Student B

1 Ask for directions to the bank. Which colour circle is it?
2 Give directions to the bookshop.
   We are at the station. Go down Prince Street. Turn left at the park into Regent Street. Go past the hotel and the cinema. Go straight on. The bookshop is on the left between the museum and the restaurant.

10   Vocabulary p.98

Student B

Match the airlines and the nationalities. Check your answers with Student A.

Brazilian   American   Dutch   Polish   Japanese

1 LOT
2 Cathay Pacific   Chinese
3 Delta
4 EasyJet   British
5 All Nippon Airways
6 Aeroflot   Russian
7 TAM
8 Iberia   Spanish
9 KLM
10 Alitalia   Italian

     Example   **Student B** Is LOT an American airline?
                Student A No, it isn't. It's …

Scripts

1

1.1
1 A Hello, I'm Adriana Gilberto.
   B Hi, I'm Ken Scott.
   A Welcome to the Water Conference.
2 A Hi. My name's Tim Brown.
   B Hello. I'm Li Qin.
   A Welcome to the Water Conference, Li Qin.
3 A Hi. I'm Aziz Mohamed.
   B Hello. My name's Giovanni Fratelli.
4 A Hello. My name's Irina Ivanova. I'm from St Petersburg in Russia.
   B Pleased to meet you, Irina. I'm Jean and this is Marie. We're from Saint-Louis in Senegal.

1.2
T=Tim, A=Adriana
T OK. Let's check the people at the conference. This is Ken Scott.
A That's right.
T He's from Boston in the United States.
A Yes. And this is Li Qin.
T Yes. She's from Chengdu.
A Chengdu?
T Yes. It's in China.
A And this is Jean and Marie Bouvier. They're from Dakar in Senegal.
T Dakar? I think it's Saint-Louis.
A Oh, yes. You're right. Saint-Louis.

1.3
I am   I'm
You are   You're
He is   He's
She is   She's
It is   It's
We are   We're
They are   They're

1.4
zero, one, two, three, four, five, six, seven, eight, nine, ten

1.5
1 A AlphaCo, please.
   B They're in building seven.
   A Thanks.
2 A Good morning. Brand Link, please.
   B Building five.
   A Thanks.
3 A Good morning.
   B Morning.
   A Casino Tec, please.
   B They're in building number three.
   A Thanks.
   B You're welcome.
4 A Good morning. Global, please.
   B They're in building nine.
   A OK. Thanks.
5 A Good morning.
   B Hot Designs, please. Number nine?
   A No. Number ten.
   B Oh, thank you.
   A You're welcome.

1.6
6 A Good morning.
   B Good morning. Nostrum, please.
   A They're in building four.
   B Thanks.
   A That's OK.

1.6
1 This is a message for Casino Tec. Please call 07963 496108.
2 For AlphaCo. Please call Tom Black on 07762 795979.
3 Hot Designs. Telephone 01865 354091. That's 01865 354091.
4 This is a call for Dan Smith at Brand Link. Please contact Sally. 07581 395563.
5 This is a message for Helen Smith at Nostrum. Please call Melanie on 01865 990312.

1.7
07963 496108
07762 795979
01865 354091
07581 395563
01865 990312

1.8
A B C D E F G H I J K L M N O P Q R S T U V W X Y Z

1.9
A R Y E I G J C K W H U V

1.10
1 Los Angeles, LAX
2 Amsterdam, AMS
3 Berlin, BER
4 Cairo, CAI
5 Hong Kong, HKG
6 Mexico City, MEX
7 Lima, LIM
8 Miami, MIA
9 Caracas, CCS
10 Bangkok, BKK

1.11
A Hello, I'm Kyra Tejero.
B Can you spell that, please?
A Yes. Kyra. K-Y-R-A.
B K-Y-R-A? Is that right?
A Yes. And Tejero: T-E-J-E-R-O.

1.12
1 Ajeet Singh
2 Lauren Nzunga
3 Lisa Chang
4 Charlotte Charlesworth
5 Daisuke Nakamoto
6 Klaus Schmitt

1.13
1 A=Andy, An=Angela
   A Good morning. My name's Andy Rosser.
   An Good morning, Andy. My name's Angela. Angela Teo.
   A Nice to meet you, Angela.
   An Nice to meet you too.
2 M=Martin, An=Angela, L=Lynne
   M Hi. I'm Martin Katz.
   An Pleased to meet you, Martin. I'm Angela Teo.

M Nice to meet you, Angela. This is my colleague, Lynne Murphy.
An Pleased to meet you, Lynne.
L Nice to meet you too, Angela.
3 An=Angela, F=Fernando
   An Fernando Rodriguez?
   F Yes.
   An Hello. I'm Angela Teo.
   F Oh, Angela. Very nice to meet you.
   An Very nice to meet you too, Fernando.

1.14
1 J=Jess, T=Tariq
   J Good morning.
   T Good morning.
   J How are you?
   T Great. And you?
   J Fine, thanks.
2 R=Ross, J=Jess
   R Hello.
   J Hi. How are things?
   R Good. And you?
   J Pretty good.

1.15
1 020 6679 2134
2 0113 901 8779
3 (34) 94 719 0004
4 (44) 1865 548222
5 020 8813 0809

1.16
1 A H J K
2 B C D E G P T V
3 F L M N S X Z
4 I Y
5 O
6 Q U W
7 R

1.17
1 A B C D E
2 L O M F N
3 L H A K J
4 I E Y
5 T M E C G

1.18
1 A My name's Bryan.
   B Is that with an 'i' or a 'y'?
   A With a 'y'. B-R-Y-A-N.
2 A I'm Bill Brown.
   B Can you spell that, please?
   A Yes, sure. B-R-O-W-N.
3 A I'm Sarah Connery.
   B Can you spell that, please?
   A Of course, it's C-O-N-N-E-R-Y.
   B Thanks.

1.19
1 Barbara B-A-R-B-A-R-A
   Losue L-O-S-U-E
2 Anthony A-N-T-H-O-N-Y
   Eagle E-A-G-L-E
3 Mahmoud M-A-H-M-O-U-D
   Al Kouz A-L K-O-U-Z
4 Mandy M-A-N-D-Y
   Rowland R-O-W-L-A-N-D

2

2.1
A=Adriana, M=Mona
A Hello, I'm Adriana.
M Hello, I'm Mona Apaydin.
A Are you from the Emirates, Mona?
M Yes, I am. I'm from Dubai.
A Great. And are you a designer?
M No, I'm not. I'm an architect.
A Welcome to the conference.
M Thank you.

T=Tim, To=Toshihiko, K=Kimiko
T Hello, my name's Tim.
To Hello, Tim. I'm Toshihiko.
K And I'm Kimiko.
T Are you from Japan?
K Yes, we are.
T And are you from Tokyo?
To No, we're not from Tokyo. We're from Osaka. I'm a designer.
K And I'm a project manager.

2.2
T=Tim, A=Adriana
T Is Yvette a teacher?
A Yvette Bonnier? No, she isn't. She's an engineer. And she's from France.
T OK. And Edmundo?
A Edmundo Gonzales?
T Yes.
A He's a doctor from Spain.
T Is he married?
A No, he isn't.

2.3
1 **A=Adriana, Y=Yvette**
   A Hello, I'm Adriana. Are you Yvette Bonnier?
   Y Yes, I am.
   A Are you from France, Yvette?
   Y Yes, I am.
   A And are you a teacher?
   Y No, I'm not. I'm an engineer.
2 **A=Adriana, To=Toshihiko, K=Kimoko**
   A Are you from Tokyo?
   To No, we're not. We're from Osaka.
   A So, are you both engineers?
   K No, we're not. I'm a project manager.
   To And I'm a designer.

2.4
eleven, twelve, thirteen, fourteen, fifteen, sixteen, seventeen, eighteen, nineteen, twenty

2.5
twenty, thirty, forty, fifty, sixty, seventy, eighty, ninety, a hundred

2.6
1 thirteen   thirty
2 fourteen   forty
3 fifteen   fifty
4 sixteen   sixty
5 seventeen   seventy
6 eighteen   eighty
7 nineteen   ninety

2.7
1 thirty
2 fourteen
3 fifty
4 sixteen
5 seventeen

6 eighty
7 ninety

2.8
seventy, seventy-one, seventy-two, seventy-three, seventy-four, seventy-five, seventy-six, seventy-seven, seventy-eight, seventy-nine, eighty

2.9
1 The temperature in Shanghai is 18 degrees.
2 The temperature in Sydney is 27 degrees.
3 The temperature in Moscow is 4 degrees.
4 The temperature in Brasilia is 28 degrees.
5 The temperature in London is 11 degrees.
6 The temperature in Dubai is 36 degrees.
7 The temperature in Paris is 13 degrees.
8 The temperature in Mecca is 40 degrees.

2.10
1 It's ten o'clock.
2 It's ten thirty.
3 It's ten forty-five.
4 It's eleven o'clock.
5 It's eleven fifteen.

2.11
1 It's eight o'clock.
2 It's one thirty.
3 It's four forty-five.
4 It's five fifteen.
5 It's nine o'clock.

2.12
A=Adriana
A Good morning. Welcome to Day 2 of the conference. The talk 'Water Problems in Africa' is at nine fifteen. Welcome Professor Fahima Rani.
At ten o'clock you can ask Professor Rani questions.
At ten thirty it's the coffee break in the conference room.
At eleven o'clock groups A to E have workshops in rooms nine to thirteen.
Lunch is at twelve thirty in the restaurant.
At one forty-five groups F to J have workshops in rooms nine to thirteen.
Tea is at three fifteen.
At three forty-five we have workshop feedback.
At five o'clock it's question time: 'Ask the scientists'.
Have a good day, everybody.

2.13
A Excuse me. What time is the coffee break?
B At ten thirty.
A Thanks.
B You're welcome.

2.14
V=Volker, L=Laura
V Hello. My name's Volker. Volker Ziegert.
L Hello, I'm Laura Zumeta. Are you here for the conference?
V Yes, I'm a trainer.
L Are you on the schedule today?
V Yes, at one forty-five for a workshop.

L Great! Are you from Germany, Volker?
V No, I'm not. I'm from Austria. I work for Watertime …
L Watertime?
V Yes, it's a research company in Salzburg.
L Are you a scientist?
V No, I'm a project manager.
L So, you live in Salzburg?
V No, I'm from Austria, but I live and work in Lagos, in Nigeria.
L Really?
V Yes, it's great. I travel a lot too. I travel to Asia, Europe, and South America for my job. And you, Laura? …

2.15
L=Laura, E=Eva, V=Volker
K Eva, this is Volker Ziegert. He's from Austria.
E Nice to meet you, Volker. I'm Eva Gonzalez.
V Nice to meet you too, Eva.
L Volker works for Watertime Research Company. He's a project manager. He lives and works in Nigeria.
E Really?
L Eva is a teacher. She works for WTL. It's a charity. It's in Argentina, but she lives in Peru.
V How interesting!

2.16
J=Jack, R=Ronaldo
J Hello, I'm Jack Nutley.
R Hi, I'm Ronaldo Tejero. Nice to meet you.
J Nice to meet you too. Are you from Spain, Ronaldo?
R No, I'm from Portugal. I live in Faro, but I travel to Spain for my job.
J Really?
R Yes, I work for Get Away! It's a travel company. I'm a director. And you?
J Well, I'm from Canada. I live and work in Toronto. I'm the manager of the Intercontinental Hotel in Toronto. Here's my card.
R Thanks.

2.17
You're not. You aren't.
He's not. He isn't.
We're not. We aren't.
They're not. They aren't.

2.18
1 18
2 71
3 66
4 50
5 31
6 14

2.19
1 six ten
2 six thirty
3 six forty
4 six forty-five
5 six twenty
6 six fifteen
7 six fifty

2.20
Good morning. Welcome to Day 3 of the conference. So, today, the workshops are at nine ten for groups A to E.

Coffee break is at ten forty.
The talk by Doctor Fiona Hofer is at eleven fifteen.
Lunch is at one o'clock.
Workshops for groups F to J are at two thirty.
Tea is at four o'clock.
We say goodbye here at four forty.
Enjoy your day.

2.21 ●))
Hello. My name's Satoko Yamamoto.
I'm from Japan, but I live in Swords.
It's in Ireland. I work for Adecco. It's a recruitment company. I'm a recruitment officer. I travel to America and Japan for work. It's great!

2.22 ●))
Hi. My name's Andreas Westermann. I'm from Germany, but I live in Switzerland, in Zurich.
I work for the Swiss finance company Credit Suisse. I'm an accounts manager. I travel mainly to France and the UK. It's a really interesting job.

3

3.1 ●))
R=Rick, Y=Yoon Kwon
R Good morning. MyOffice. How can I help you?
Y Good morning. My name's Yoon Kwon. I'm from GIIR. My company wants to rent offices in New York.
R OK.
Y Could you tell me about the centre on Sixth Avenue?
R Certainly. In the centre there is a reception area. Then there's a meeting room, and there are five offices.
Y Is there an elevator?
R Yes, there is.
Y OK. Excellent. And parking?
R In the basement of the building there is a car park with spaces for ten cars.
Y Great. How about internet access?
R There is a high-speed internet connection.
Y OK. And is there a coffee shop?
R Unfortunately, there isn't a coffee shop in the centre. But there is a kitchen with coffee and tea facilities.
Y And what is there near the centre?
R Near the centre, there are some very good restaurants and shops. And there's a train station very nearby. But there aren't any banks, just ATMs.
Y OK. Thank you for your help.
R My pleasure.

3.2 ●))
Y=Yoon, D=Director
Y Good morning. I have the information about the MyOffice centre in Manhattan.
D Oh, good.
Y There are five offices.
D Great. Are there any meeting rooms?
Y Yes, there is. There's one.
D Right. And is there a reception?
Y Yes, there is.

D And internet access?
Y Yes, there's a high-speed internet connection.
D OK. And is there a car park in the building?
Y Yes, there is. In the basement.
D Excellent. How about near the centre? Are there any restaurants nearby?
Y Yes, there are lots of restaurants.
D And is there a train station?
Y Yes, there's a train station very near the centre.
D Are there any banks?
Y No, there aren't any near the office. But there's an ATM in the next building.
D OK. Thanks, Yoon. Good job.

3.3 ●))
paper
telephone
computer
books
pencils
pens
Post-its
paperclips
mouse
desk
keyboard
diary
drawer
chair

3.4 ●))
I=Interviewer, B=Barbara
I So, Barbara, this is the office?
B Yes, and this is my workstation.
I Great. So, can you describe your workstation for me?
B Of course. There's a computer, a mouse and a keyboard, and a telephone. And there's a chair. Umm … There're two drawers.
I And is there anything in the drawers?
B Yes, in the drawers there're some pens and pencils. What else? There's my diary.
I Is there any paper?
B No, there isn't any paper, and there aren't any paperclips. Oh, there're lots of Post-its too.

3.5 ●))
coffee, espresso, tea, apple juice, mineral water, orange juice, cheese sandwich, tuna sandwich, chocolate cake, plain yoghurt, fruit yoghurt

3.6 ●))
N=Nick, M=Mona, K=Kim, Nt=Note
N Would you like something to drink, Mona?
M Yes, please.
N What would you like?
M Is there any espresso?
N Yes, there is.
M OK. An espresso, please.
N Right.
M Thank you.
N Would you like something to eat, Kim?
K Yes, please.
N What would you like?
K I'd like a sandwich, please.
N OK. Cheese or tuna?
K Cheese, please.

N What would you like, Note?
Nt I'd like some apple juice, please.
N I'm sorry. There isn't any apple juice. There's orange.
Nt OK. An orange juice, please.
N Fine. Would you like something to eat?
Nt No, thanks.

3.7 ●))
Would you like something to eat?
Yes, please.
What would you like?
I'd like a yoghurt, please.
Plain or fruit?
Fruit, please.

3.8 ●))
There's a restaurant.
There're two coffee shops.
There isn't a restaurant.
There aren't any offices.
Is there a gym?
Yes, there is.
No, there isn't.
Are there any banks?
Yes, there are.
No, there aren't.

3.9 ●))
restaurants
rooms
offices

3.10 ●))
rooms, toilets, offices, banks, car parks, centres, managers, bosses, conferences

3.11 ●))
J=June, Je=Jeanine
J Would you like a drink, Jeanine?
Je Yes, please.
J What would you like?
Je Orange juice, please.
J Would you like something to eat? There are biscuits or cake.
Je No, thanks.

4

4.1 ●))
credit cards
a mobile phone
a passport
plane tickets
money
documents
a gift
business cards
a laptop

4.2 ●))
M=Mike, E=Ella
M Hi, Ella. How are you?
E Fine thanks, Mike.
M Have you got everything?
E Yes, I have. Don't worry! I've got my passport, laptop, credit cards, and money.
M Has Becky got the plane tickets?
E No, she hasn't. She's got the code on her mobile phone.
M OK. Have you got the business cards?
E Becky, have we got the business cards? (Yeah.) Yes, we have.
M Great. Have you got the documents?

E   No, I haven't. Becky, have you got the documents? (Yeah.) Yes, she has.

M   OK, have a good trip.

E   Thanks.

M   Oh, and have you got a gift for Mr Yamamoto?

E   No, we haven't! But they've got British souvenirs in the shops at the airport …

4.3 ●))

Monday, Tuesday, Wednesday, Thursday, Friday, Saturday, Sunday

4.4 ●))

January, February, March, April, May, June, July, August, September, October, November, December

4.5 ●))

first, second, third, fourth, fifth, sixth, seventh, eighth, ninth, tenth, eleventh, twelfth, thirteenth, fourteenth, fifteenth, sixteenth, seventeenth, eighteenth, nineteenth, twentieth, twenty-first, thirtieth

4.6 ●))

the fifteenth of October
the twenty-third of October
October the nineteenth
October the thirtieth

4.7 ●))

2014   1914   1814   2001   1901   1801

4.8 ●))

R=Receiver, C=Caller, L=Lisa Chang

R   Good morning, KLF Limited. How can I help you?

C   Good morning. Could I speak to Lisa Chang, please?

R   Certainly. Can I take your name, please?

C   Yes. It's Juan Carlos Rodriguez.

R   Thank you, Mr Rodriguez. Please hold the line.

C   Thank you.

L   Lisa Chang speaking.

C   Hi, Lisa. It's Juan Carlos from Novotec.

L   Oh, hi Juan. How are you?

C   Fine, thanks. I'm calling about our meeting on Monday …

4.9 ●))

J=Jacques, K=Karla

J   Hello, is that Karla? It's Jacques Brennard here.

K   Hi, Jacques. How can I help you?

J   Are you free on Wednesday morning for a meeting?

K   Let me check … I'm sorry, I'm busy on Wednesday morning. How about in the afternoon?

J   Yes, the afternoon is OK. How about two o'clock?

K   Yes, two o'clock is fine with me.

J   Great. So my office on Wednesday at two o'clock.

K   OK. See you then.

J   Thanks! Bye

4.10 ●))

I've got a laptop.
I haven't got a laptop.
He's got a credit card.
He hasn't got a credit card.
She's got a business card.
She hasn't got a business card.
It's got a shop.

It hasn't got a shop.
We've got the documents.
We haven't got the documents.
They've got a gift.
They haven't got a gift.

4.11 ●))

1   A   The meeting is on the thirtieth of April.
    B   The thirteenth?
    A   No. Saturday the thirtieth.
2   A   The conference is on the 18th and the 19th of April.
    B   Is that a Thursday and a Friday?
    A   No, it's a Monday and a Tuesday.

4.12 ●))

January, February, March, April, May, June, July, August, September, October, November, December

4.13 ●))

1   2015
2   1915
3   2004
4   1904
5   2020
6   1920

4.14 ●))

R=Receiver, C=Caller, M=Mark

R   Good morning, Technos. How can I help you?

C   Hello. Could I speak to Mark Cooke, please?

R   Certainly. Can I take your name?

C   Yes. It's Mohamed Hanif.

R   Thank you, Mr Hanif. Please hold the line.

C   Thank you.

M   Mark Cooke speaking.

C   Hi, Mark. It's Mohamed from Novotec.

M   Oh, hi. How are you?

C   Fine, thanks. I'm calling about our meeting on Monday …

4.15 ●))

K=Katrina, L=Lucy

K   Hi, Lucy. This is Katrina.

L   Hello, Katrina.

K   Lucy, are you free on Friday?

L   Let me check. No, I'm sorry, I'm busy on Friday. How about Thursday?

K   Yes, Thursday is OK.

L   In the morning?

K   Yes. How about 9.00?

L   9.00 is fine with me.

K   Great! Let's meet in the coffee shop.

L   OK. So Thursday at 9.00 in the coffee shop.

K   Thanks, Lucy. Bye.

5

5.1 ●))

Freelancer

I=Interviewer, M=Matt

I   Does the commute take long?

M   No, it doesn't take long – about five minutes!

I   Does the coffee shop have free Wi-Fi?

M   Yes, it does. It doesn't cost anything. But I always buy lots of coffees and snacks.

I   Do you ever work in an office?

M   No, I never work in an office. I don't work for a company. I'm a freelancer.

I   Do you go to the coffee shop every day?

M   Yes, I do. Always. Weekdays and Saturdays and Sundays. But I don't work at the weekend. I just hang out with friends.

Company worker

I=Interviewer, L=Lisa

I   Do you live in Madrid?

L   No, I don't. I live in the countryside. It's great for the family but it's a long way from Madrid.

I   Does the commute take long?

L   Yes, it does. It takes about an hour by train.

I   Do you ever drive?

L   Yes, I do. Sometimes the train is late and I take the car.

I   Does the company pay?

L   No, it doesn't. I pay about 200 euros a month.

5.2

Egil Andersen comes from Norway but he lives in São Paulo in Brazil. He works for Petrobras, the Brazilian energy company. He sometimes goes to the main office in Rio de Janeiro.

He commutes three hours a day. He always gets up at 6.00 in the morning and gets home at about 9.00 at night.

He loves Brazilian food and always eats lunch at one of the local restaurants. He never eats Norwegian food. He speaks English, Norwegian, and Portuguese.

5.3 ●))

1   Pedro, how do you get to work?
    There aren't any trains where I live. So I go to work by car. It takes about 30 minutes.
2   Lynne, do you go to work by bus?
    Yes, I live near the city centre so I take the bus. It takes about 15 minutes.
3   How do you get to work, Dieter?
    To work? I go by train. It takes 30 minutes.
4   Lee, how do you get to work?
    Me? I go to work by bicycle. It's cheap and it only takes about 20 minutes.
5   How do you get to work, Narumi?
    How do I get to the office? Well, I sometimes take a taxi if I'm late.
6   Ana, do you walk to work?
    Yes. The traffic is really bad and my office isn't far, so I always go on foot. It takes about 25 minutes.
7   Christian, how do you get to work?
    I go to work by boat. There's a ferry at eight o'clock. It takes 20 minutes.
8   How do you get to work, John?
    I go to the main office in Germany every week. I live in London so it's about two hours by plane.

5.4 ●))

1   The British Airways flight for Tokyo Narita leaves Heathrow Airport at 2.45 from gate 6.
2   Could you put the bicycle back in the stand when you return?
3   The ferry to Cheung Chau leaves the Tsim Sha Tsui pier in five minutes.

4 The car park costs €3 per hour.
5 Passengers for the Prince Hotel, get off at the last bus stop in the city centre.
6 The next train for Firenze leaves platform 9 at 10.15.

5.5 ◉))
J=John, E=Elena
J Hello. John Davis speaking. Can I help you?
E Could I speak to Rob Gordon, please?
J I'm sorry. He's in a meeting at the moment. Can I take a message?
E Yes, please. Could you ask him to call me? My name's Elena Moretti. I work in the Milan office.
J Elena Moretti …
E Yes, that's E-L-E-N-A M-O-R-E-T-T-I.
J OK. Does he have your number?
E I don't think so. It's 0039.
J 0039.
E 8536.
J 8536.
E 0001, extension 45.
J 0001, extension 45. Thank you. I'll ask him to call you.
E Thank you. Bye.
J Bye.

5.6 ◉))
L=Lara, K=Kenichi
L Are you free tomorrow?
K Yes, I am. It's nice to have some time with my family.
L What do you like doing?
K I like walking.
L OK. How about visiting Holland Park? It's a great place for a walk.
K That sounds great.
L What does your wife like?
K She really likes department stores.
L OK. I suggest you go to Harvey Nichols. It's a department store near Holland Park. It's a really good place for women's fashion.
K Perfect.
L Right. And how about your daughter?
K She likes British culture. And she likes looking round art galleries.
L Then how about going to the Victoria and Albert Museum? It's a beautiful old building, and inside there are lots of paintings and photos. They've got some exhibitions of furniture and jewellery too.

5.7 ◉))
eats, lives, speaks, does, buys, gets

5.8 ◉))
1 **R=Receiver, C=Caller**
R Good morning. Gristech and Sons. Can I help you?
C Yes, good morning. Can I speak to Will Lansford, please?
R I'm sorry, he's in a meeting at the moment. Can I take a message?
C Yes, please ask him to call Tanya Hording at the Richmond Hotel.
R Of course. Could you spell your family name for me, please?
C Yes, it's H-O-R-D-I-N-G.
R Thank you, and it's the Richmond Hotel. What's the number?

C It's 0470 3332145.
R I'll ask him to call you.
C Thank you.
2 **R=Receiver, C=Caller**
R Good morning. Gristech and Sons. Can I help you?
C Good morning. Could I speak to Alisha, please?
R I'm afraid she's not in the office today.
C Oh … Could I leave a message?
R Of course. What's your name, please?
C It's Ron Olbrich. That's O-L-B-R-I-C-H.
R And your telephone number? Are you in the Netherlands?
C No, I'm in the office in Brazil. That's 0055 27 67590, extension 3.
R OK, that's 0055 27 67590, extension 3.
C Yes, thank you.
R No problem, I'll give her your message.

6

6.1 ◉))
R=Rafael, M=Maria, S=Sean, C=Carlos, A=Angela, K=Kim, D=Denis
R You're from Argentina. Do you live there now?
M No, we don't. We live in our new home in Dubai.
S Do you have a new yacht as well?
C Yes, a Volvo 60. It's beautiful – very fast and great to sail.
A Have you got a sponsor for your boat?
M Yes, we've got a very good sponsor. It's a TV company. We use its logo on our clothes and equipment. It's a big help for us.
K Do you race every month?
M Yes. Our next race is in September. It's Les Voiles de Saint-Tropez in France.
K Do you have any other interests or hobbies?
M We own a small fish restaurant near the Dubai Yacht Club. Carlos manages the restaurant and his father helps me in the kitchen. I really enjoy it.
D It sounds like you both have a very busy lifestyle.
C Yes, that's true. But Maria also likes a quiet life. For her it's good to have her private time. In the evening, she loves to read or phone her friends and her family. She speaks with them for hours!
M And Carlos sits with his friends for hours in the restaurant. He loves to talk about sailing and yachts. That's important for him!

6.2 ◉))
1 Are you from Argentina?
   Yes, I am.
2 Do you and Maria live in the Emirates?
   Yes, we do.
3 Is your new home in Dubai?
   That's right. We live in Dubai now.
4 Is your yacht very fast?
   Yes, it is.

5 Have you got your sponsor's logo on your clothes?
   Yes, we have and its logos are also on the sails of our yacht.
6 Does Carlos like to sit with his friends in your restaurant?
   Yes, he loves to sit and talk to them.
7 What does Maria do in the evening?
   She phones her friends.
8 I would like to meet you. When is your next race?
   It's in September. Come and meet us in Dubai!

6.3 ◉))
1 chips / French fries
2 burger
3 pasta
4 pizza
5 soup
6 salad
7 rice
8 noodles
9 kebabs
10 couscous
11 chicken curry
12 nan bread
13 baguette
14 croissant
15 oranges
16 bananas
17 tiramisu
18 ice cream

6.4 ◉))
The European Union currency is the euro. The currency in the USA is the dollar. In China it's the yuan. India's currency is the rupee. And in Brazil it's the real. In Japan it's the yen and in the UAE it's the dirham. And, finally, the pound is the currency in the UK.

6.5 ◉))
M=Maria, D=Daniel
M Is Paris expensive?
D Yes, it is. Prices are very high in the tourist areas.
M How much is a hotel?
D Cheap hotels near the airport cost about 90 euros. Good hotels in the centre of Paris cost around 170 euros a night. Luxury hotels cost over 200 euros.
M I'd like to stay in a good hotel, I think. How much is the flight?
D A return flight from Dubai to Paris is about 3,000 dirham.
M And how much is a taxi from Charles de Gaulle Airport to the city?
D It's between 40 and 70 euros.
M How about food?
D It's pretty expensive. About 40 euros for a lunch menu.
M OK. Can I get internet access?
D No problem. Wi-Fi is free in a lot of places in Paris.
M Great. Is the exchange rate good?
D I'm not sure. I think 10 dirham is about 2 euros.
M Right. Thanks for your help.

6.6 ◉))
R=Restaurant, H=Helen
R Bocca di Leone. How can I help you?

H I'd like to make a reservation for tonight, please.
R Certainly. For how many people?
H For two.
R For two people. And from what time?
H Seven thirty.
R Seven thirty. And your name, please?
H Yes, it's Helen Moran. M-O-R-A-N.
R Thank you very much, Ms Moran. We'll see you at 7.30.
H Thank you.

6.7 ◉))
R=Restaurant, H=Helen, W=Waiter, S=Silvio
R Good evening.
H Good evening. I have a reservation. The name is Moran.
R Ms Moran. Here we are. This way, please.
H Thank you.
…
W Are you ready to order?
S Yes, for the starter I'd like the soup, please.
H OK, I think I'll have the salad.
W Soup and salad. And for the main course?
H Do you have any vegetarian dishes?
W Yes, we have a pasta with cheese and the pizza with mushrooms.
H OK, I'll have the pasta, please.
W Very good. And for you, sir?
S I'll have the pizza, please.
W And what would you like to drink?
S Water for me, please.
H A bottle of water and a glass of orange juice, please.
W Fine.
H Oh and can we have some bread and olives, please?
W Of course.

6.8 ◉))
H=Helen, S=Silvio, W=Waiter
H How's your soup, Silvio?
S It's OK. It's a bit salty. How's your salad?
H It's delicious – very fresh.
…
S How's the pasta?
H Pretty good. It's a bit soft. How about your pizza?
S It's really good.
…
W How was your meal? Was everything OK?
S Yes, really good, thanks.
W Would you like a dessert?
S No, thank you.
H Not for me, thanks. Would you like a coffee?
S No, thanks. We need to get back to the office.
H You're right. Could we have the bill, please?
W Yes, certainly.

6.9 ◉))
I have breakfast at seven o'clock. For breakfast I have tea with bread and butter. Sometimes I have an egg as well. I have lunch at one o'clock in a small restaurant near my office. I have chicken with rice or beef with vegetables. I eat dinner at home. I like cooking and my friends come to my house to eat. I have dinner at six o'clock. I cook rice with chicken or fish. For dessert I make my own ice cream or have baklava, a kind of pastry.

7

7.1 ◉))
R=Reporter, S=Shirin
R So, Shirin, what kind of company do you work for?
S I work for an airline.
R Where is the main office?
S At Doha International Airport in Qatar.
R And what do you do?
S I'm a cabin attendant.
R Where do you fly?
S I fly all around the world – New York, Shanghai, Paris, Cape Town, and so on.
R Which is your favourite city?
S I love Paris. It's great for shopping and restaurants and sightseeing. Everything.
R How many times do you fly in a month?
S It depends. About eight or ten.
R And when do you have a break?
S I have a break after every flight. Usually one or two days. I get a longer break after a long flight like Tokyo or Buenos Aires.
R Who do you work with?
S On a flight I work with a team of about ten cabin crew and three flight crew.
R When is your next flight?
S After this interview.

7.2 ◉))
S=Sylvia, G=Gordon
S Hi. I'm Sylvia.
G Hello, I'm Gordon.
S Nice to meet you, Gordon. Which company do you work for?
G I work for STN Airlines.
S What do you do?
G I'm a pilot.
S Where do you work?
G My base is Heathrow Airport, in London.
S How many times do you fly in a week?
G I fly to Europe so I do two flights a day, five days a week.
S So, about ten flights a week?
G Yes.
S Who do you fly with?
G I fly with just one other pilot, the first officer. And of course the cabin crew.
S When is your next flight?
G On Saturday.

7.3 ◉))
monorail
departures
information desk

shops
parking
toilets
security
taxi stand
restaurants
arrivals
newsagent's
baggage claim
bookshop
trolleys
check-in desks

7.4 ◉))
1 Hi Katie, this is Kim. I'm in arrivals. I can't see you, but I'm at the bookshop.
2 Hello, this is a message for Mr Schmidt. Please meet your driver at the information desk in the arrivals hall. Many thanks.
3 Hello. Keiko? It's me, Maria. I'm in the car park. Can you meet me at the check-in desks on the upper floor? Bye.
4 Hi David, I'm going to the newsagent's in the arrivals hall. See you there.

7.5 ◉))
1 seat
2 safety belt
3 folding table
4 overhead locker
5 window blind
6 blanket
7 lights
8 remote control

7.6 ◉))
CA=cabin attendant, P=passenger
1 CA Excuse me, sir. Could you close your window blind, please? We're turning the lights down now.
   P   Oh, sure.
2 CA Which would you like, madam? The chicken or the pasta?
   P   Could I have the pasta, please? And could I have another tomato juice?
   CA Certainly.
3 CA How can I help?
   P   Could you show me how to use the remote control?
   CA OK. Just press this button here to start with …
4 CA Could you fasten your safety belt? We're going to land in a few minutes.
   P   I'm sorry. I was asleep.
   CA No problem.
5 P   Could I have a blanket, please?
   CA I'll see if we have any more.
6 CA Could you put your bag in the overhead locker?
   P   It's rather heavy. Could you give me a hand?
   CA Actually, that is too heavy …
7 P   Have you got any more in-flight magazines?
   CA Certainly. Would you like a newspaper as well?
   P   That would be great.
8 CA Could you go back to your seat, please, sir?

7.7 ●))

1 A Good evening. Could I see your boarding card, please?
  B Here you are.
  A Thank you. You're in row 15.
2 A Could you put your bag under the seat, please?
  B OK.
3 A Sorry. Could I have a glass of mineral water?
  B Certainly, sir. With ice?
  A Yes, please.
4 A Could you go back to your seat and fasten your safety belt?
  B Sure. Could I get my sweater first?
  A OK.
5 A Have you got any more menus?
  B Yes. I'll bring you one in just a moment.
6 A Could you check my folding table? I think it's broken.
  B OK. I'll ask the Chief Purser to look at it for you.

8

8.1 ●))

The Savoy Hotel opened in London about 120 years ago. It was the first luxury hotel in England. Many famous people and celebrities stayed there. Elizabeth Taylor, Charlie Chaplin, and the Beatles were all guests.

The first famous guest was the French artist, Monet. He painted pictures of the River Thames from his hotel room. Oscar Wilde, the Irish writer, lived in the hotel for about a month. Fred Astaire danced on the roof of the hotel. Frank Sinatra played the piano in the American Bar. In the 60s, Bob Dylan stayed there and made a music video next to the hotel.

8.2 ●))

I=Interviewer, J=James
I James, do you like your job in the new Savoy Hotel?
J Yes, I love it here. It's a very special place.
I Can you give us some information about the Savoy?
J Certainly. It opened in 1889 and it was the first hotel with electric lights … *and* hot and cold water in the bathrooms. It had electric lifts as well.
I Did famous people and royalty stay here?
J Yes, they did. Hollywood stars like Elizabeth Taylor, John Wayne, Marilyn Monroe, and Marlon Brando. Elizabeth Taylor loved the hotel. She stayed here four times with four different husbands.
I I see!
J And Queen Elizabeth was a visitor.
I Did the Queen stay here?
J No, she didn't. She was here for a party and met her future husband, Prince Philip, here.
I When did the hotel close?
J It closed in 2007.
I Why did the hotel close?

J The new owners, Fairmont Hotels and Resorts, wanted to upgrade the whole hotel.
I How much did it cost?
J The project cost 220 million pounds.
I Is the new hotel open now?
J Yes, it opened in 2010.

8.3 ●))

1 reception
2 bags
3 key card
4 credit card
5 registration form
6 reservation
7 passport
8 lift

8.4 ●))

1 bed
2 television
3 wardrobe
4 window
5 light
6 bathroom
7 bath
8 shower
9 towel
10 door

8.5 ●))

R=Reception, M=Milena
R Hello. Hotel Maurice. How can I help you?
M Hello. I'd like to change my reservation details.
R Certainly. Could I have your name, please?
M Milena Scott.
R I'm sorry. Could you repeat that, please?
M Milena Scott.
R Is that with two 'l's?
M No one 'l'
R M-I-L-E-N-A.
M That's correct.
R And Scot with one 't'.
M No, two 't's.
R I'm very sorry.
M That's OK. Could I change the booking to three nights?
R Let me just check. Is that from Monday the 15th August to Thursday the 18th?
M No, I'd like to stay from Sunday the 14th to Wednesday the 17th.
R I see. So, Sunday the 14th to Wednesday the 17th.
M That's right. And I'd like a double room, not a single room.
R A double room. OK. Let me just check the availability. A double room is 315 euros per night. Is that OK?
M I'm sorry, is that 350 or 315?
R That's 315.
M OK, that's fine.
R OK, so your new booking is for three nights from Sunday the 14th to Wednesday the 17th for a double room at 315 euros per night. And your new confirmation number is 89917.
M I'm sorry, it's a bit noisy. Could you say that again, please?
R Yes, your new confirmation number is 89917.

M 89917.
R That's right.
M Thank you very much.
R Thank you. Goodbye.
M Goodbye.

8.6 ●))

A Could I have your name, please?
B Milena Scott.
A I'm sorry. Could you repeat that, please?
B Milena Scott.
A Is that with two 'l's?
B No, one 'l'.
A M-I-L-E-N-A.
B That's correct.
A A double room is 315 euros per night. Is that OK?
B I'm sorry, is that 350 or 315?
A That's 315.
B I'm sorry, it's a bit noisy. Could you say that again, please?
A Yes, your new confirmation number is 89917.

8.7 ●))

R=Reception, Ra=Rachel Young
R Good evening. How can I help you?
Ra Good evening. I'd like to check in, please.
R Certainly. Do you have a reservation?
Ra Yes.
R Could I have your name, please?
Ra It's Rachael Young.
R OK, so you have a double room for three nights. Is that correct?
Ra Yes, that's right.
R OK. Could you fill in the registration form, please?
Ra OK. … Here you are.
R Thank you. Do you have your passport and credit card?
Ra Yes. Here you are.
R Thank you. You're in room 306 on the third floor. Here is your key card.
Ra Thanks.
R Have you got any bags?
Ra Yes, I've got two.
R Would you like the porter to take them to your room?
Ra No, that's OK. Is there a lift?
R Yes, it's over there on the right. Enjoy your stay.

8.8 ●))

R=Reception, Ra=Rachel Young
R Good morning. Can I help you?
Ra Yes, I'd like to check out, please. Room 306.
R Ms Young?
Ra That's right.
R Have you got your key card, Ms Young?
Ra Of course. Here it is.
R Did you use your minibar?
Ra Yes, I had a mineral water last night.
R OK. One moment. Yes, here's your bill. How would you like to pay?
Ra Credit card, please.
R Of course.
Ra Here's my card.
R Thank you. Can you check the amount and enter your pin number?
Ra Yes, sure.
R Thank you. And here's your receipt.

Goodbye, Ms Young. See you again soon, we hope.

Ra Thank you. Goodbye.

8.9 ◉))

R=Reception, Z=Dr Ziegert

R Good morning.

Z Good morning. I have a reservation.

R Could I have your name, please?

Z Dr Ziegert.

R Is it a single room just for tonight?

Z Yes, that's right.

R Could you fill in the registration form, please?

Z Yes of course.

R Do you have your passport and a credit card?

Z Yes, here you are.

R Thanks. Here's your key card, Dr Ziegert. You're in room 204. That's on the second floor. The lift is over there.

8.10 ◉))

lived
danced
started

8.11 ◉))

danced, started, painted, lived, stayed, filmed, opened, worked, finished, played, invented, moved

9

9.1 ◉))

A Can you tell us a bit more about Vin's amazing journey?

B Yes, of course.

A How did he make breakfast?

B He made his breakfast with a small gas stove.

A And where did he eat lunch?

B He ate some of his meals in cafés and motels on the road.

A Where did he sleep?

B He slept in a very small tent.

A What did he take with him?

B He took two mobile phones, two video cameras, a cup and spoon, a sleeping bag, and a few other things like medicine.

A Did he take any clothes?

B Yes, he took a shirt, shorts, and pants.

A Is that all?

B Yes. He didn't have space for more clothes.

A What sort of bike did he ride?

B He rode a Genesis racing bike. It's very light and fast.

A What did he see and do?

B He saw lots of beautiful scenery, especially in places like Thailand and Indonesia. He had a lot of experiences, some good, some bad. You can read about them on his website.

A Was it dangerous?

B Sometimes. Cycling was very dangerous in Rajasthan in India.

A Why did he do it?

B He did it to make money for a charity.

A How much did he make?

B He made about £18,000.

A That's amazing.

9.2 ◉))

A Where is the library?

B It's on Ocean Road, between the bank and the post office.

A Is there a bookshop in town?

B Yes. It's on Park Road, opposite the cinema.

A Where's the hotel?

B It's at the end of Ocean Road, next to the restaurant.

A Is there a supermarket?

B Yes. It's on the corner of Ocean Road and Park Road, opposite the post office.

9.3 ◉))

A Good morning. I'm Ajeet Singh from Tata Motors. I have a meeting with Ms Jensen.

B Good morning, Mr Singh. I'm Pat Dawson, Ms Jensen's PA. Nice to meet you.

A Nice to meet you too, Pat.

B How was your flight?

A It was quite long, about 12 hours. But the service was very good.

B Good. And how is the hotel?

A It's near your office, and it's very comfortable.

B Excellent. Would you like a drink?

A Yes, I'll have a coffee, please.

B No problem. With milk and sugar?

A Just milk, please.

B OK. … So, shall we go through your schedule …?

A OK. I have a copy with me.

B That's great. Your meeting with Ms Jensen is at three o'clock.

A That's right. Three o'clock. Is the meeting in this office?

B No, it's in the main meeting room. Can I help you with anything else?

A No, I don't think so.

B OK. Please come this way.

A Thank you very much. It's my first time here …

9.4 ◉))

1 **A** Excuse me. Where is the …?
  B It's on Park Street. Go straight on, past Station Hill Road. Then turn right at the coffee shop into Park Street. It's on the left, next to the chemist.
  A Thank you.

2 **A** Excuse me. How do I get to the …?
  B Go down this road to the end. Turn left and it's on the right, just before the sports centre.
  A Thank you.

3 **A** Hi. Is there a … near here?
  B Yes, there is. Go down Queen's Road. Then turn left at the cinema into Station Hill Road. It's at the end on the right.
  A Thank you.

10

10.1 ◉))

This morning, I'm going to book my flight, a return flight from London to Hong Kong. I'm going to fly Cathay Pacific this time. People say the food and service are really good. Then I'm going to email Yiyi Chen in Hong Kong. She's going to meet me at Chek Lap Kok Airport, so I'm going to send her the flight details.

Tomorrow morning, I'm going to call Joseph Nolan in Hong Kong to talk about my trip. He's going to arrange a meeting with our new partners, DesignHK. They are a design company who are going to design some of our new products. I'm going to invite everyone from DesignHK for a nice dinner. The restaurant I went to last year was terrible, so I'm going to ask Joseph for some suggestions.

I'm going to get some Hong Kong dollars from the bank. I've got a credit card but cash is really useful for taxis and snacks and things. I'm going to buy some new summer clothes because it's going to be hot in Hong Kong. And finally, my Chinese is really bad, so I'm going to learn ten new phrases and practise them on the journey.

10.2 ◉))

1 Spain   Spanish
2 Germany   German
3 Sweden   Swedish
4 Japan   Japanese
5 South Korea   Korean
6 Italy   Italian
7 the USA   American
8 France   French
9 Britain   British
10 Switzerland   Swiss

10.3 ◉))

1 Gucci is an Italian company. It makes bags.
2 Vodafone is a British company. It makes mobile phones.
3 McDonald's is an American company. It makes burgers.
4 Zara is a Spanish company. It makes clothes.
5 Ikea is a Swedish company. It makes furniture.
6 Perrier is a French company. It makes mineral water.
7 Apple is an American company. It makes laptops.
8 Toyota is a Japanese company. It makes cars.
9 Rolex is a Swiss company. It makes watches.
10 Adidas is a German company. It makes running shoes.

10.4 ◉))

Poland   Polish
China   Chinese
Russia   Russian
Brazil   Brazilian
Holland   Dutch

10.5 ●))

1 **K=Kay, J=Joseph**

K Bye, Joseph. And thanks for
   everything.
J You're welcome! I'll be in touch again
   about the DesignHK project.
K Great.
J Have a good flight.
K Thanks. Bye!

2 **C= Claudia, M=Mario**

C Goodbye, Mario. It was nice to see
   you again. I hope you have a safe
   journey home.
M Thank you.
C See you again next month.
M I look forward to it. Goodbye.
C Goodbye.

3 **A=Antonia, M=Maia**

A Bye, Maia. It was lovely to meet you.
M Yes, it was great working together.
A I look forward to working with you
   again.
M Me too. Bye, Antonia.

4 **C=Claire, I=Ian**

C Thank you very much for coming.
   Your presentation was very
   interesting.
I My pleasure.
C I'll call you next week.
I Thank you. Bye for now.
C Bye.

10.6 ●))

O=Ms Oxendon, S=Ms Sasaki

O Goodbye, Shiho. I hope you have a safe
   journey home.
S Thank you. And thank you for
   everything.
O You're welcome.
S Please say thank you to Karl from me.
O I will. See you next summer!
S Goodbye.
O Goodbye.

Answer key

1

Grammar pp.6–7

2 Ken Scott – USA
Tim Brown – UK
Adriana Gilberto – Brazil
Li Qin – China
Irina Ivanova – Russia
Jean and Marie Bouvier – Senegal
Aziz Mohamed –Saudi Arabia
Giovanni Fratelli – Italy

3 2 She's   4 They're
3 It's   5 You're

Focus

Long form	Short form
I am	I'm
You are	**You're**
He is	**He's**
She **is**	She's
It is	It's
We are	**We're**
They are	They're

We use *I* + **am** with our names.
We use *am* / *is* / *are* + **from** with our country.

4 1 I'm; I'm; We're   5 It's
2 She's   6 He's; is
3 you're   7 's
4 They're

Vocabulary p.8

2 0 – zero, 1 – one, 2 – two, 3 – three, 4 – four, 5 – five, 6 – six, 7 – seven, 8 – eight, 9 – nine, 10 – ten

3 1 e   2 a   3 b   4 f   5 h   6 j   7 c
8 d   9 i   10 g

4 2 5   5 10
3 3   6 4
4 9

5 2 07762 795979   4 07581 395563
3 01865 354091   5 01865 990312

Work skills p.9

2 A R Y E I G J C K W H U V

3 2 AMS   7 LIM
3 BER   8 MIA
4 CAI   9 CCS
5 HKG   10 BKK
6 MEX

Functions pp.10–11

1 Andy Rosser   Lynne Murphy
Martin Katz   Fernando Rodriguez

2 1 My name's; meet
2 I'm; This is
3 Hello; Very nice

4 1 Good morning. ✓   How are you? ✓   Great. ✓
Fine, thanks. ✓
2 Hi. ✓   How are things? ✓   Good. ✓   Pretty good. ✓

Focus

Introductions	Greeting friends and colleagues
My name's Angela.	Hi.
Pleased to meet you.	How are you?
Good morning.	Good morning.
Nice to meet you.	How are things?
This is Andy Rosser.	Hello.
Very nice to meet you.	Fine, thanks.
Hello.	
I'm Martin Katz.	

5 1 e   2 f   3 h   4 g   5 a   6 b   7 d
8 c

6
Jane	Oh, good afternoon, Jia Li. I'm Jane Black.	2
Jia Li	Good afternoon. My name's Jia Li Woo.	1
Roy	And you. Welcome to the UK.	6
Jia Li	Pleased to meet you too, Roy.	5
Jia Li	Nice to meet you, Jane.	3
Jane	And you too. And this is my colleague, Roy Batty.	4

Review

Grammar pp.12–13

1 2 You are welcome.   5 We are from Medina.
3 He is Martin Katz.   6 They are from Saudi Arabia.
4 It is in the UK.   7 My name is Mamdouh.

2 2 We're   4 He's
3 She's; It's   5 They're

3 2 Where is that?   5 Where are you from?
3 He is from Dubai.   6 We are from Saudi Arabia.
4 What is your name?   7 They are from Argentina.

Vocabulary p.13

1 2 six   5 seven
3 eight   6 five
4 nine

2 1 two   6 eight
2 five   7 four
3 six   8 seven
4 nine   9 three
5 ten   10 one

3 See script 1.15.

Work skills p.14

1 1 J   2 E, P   3 N, Z   4 Y   6 U

2 1 A   2 O   3 L   4 E   5 M

3 1 a   2 a   3 b

Functions pp.14–15

1 2 bI   3 dG   4 eI   5 aG

2 1 Hi / Hello.
2 Great / Fine, thanks.

3 1 name's   4 Tina
2 meet you   5 too
3 This is

4 A 3   B 2

2

Grammar pp.16–17

1 1 the Emirates
2 Dubai
3 architect
4 Osaka
5 designer
6 project manager

2 1 France
2 engineer
3 Spain
4 doctor

3 1 b   2 a   3 a   4 b   5 a

Focus
To make a question, we use **Are** + *you*; **Is** + *he, she, it.*
To make negatives, we use *I* + **am** + *not*; *he, she, it* + **is** + *not*; *you, we, they* + **are** + *not.*

4 1 1 I'm   2 Are you   3 I am   4 Are you
5 I am   6 are you   7 I'm not   8 I'm
2 1 Are you   2 we're not   3 we're not

Vocabulary p.18

2 11 – eleven, 12 – twelve, 13 – thirteen, 14 – fourteen, 15 – fifteen, 16 – sixteen, 17 – seventeen, 18 – eighteen, 19 – nineteen, 20 – twenty

4 20 – twenty, 30 – thirty, 40 – forty, 50 – fifty, 60 – sixty, 70 – seventy, 80 – eighty, 90 – ninety, 100 – a hundred

6 1 30 thirty
2 14 fourteen
3 50 fifty
4 16 sixteen
5 17 seventeen
6 80 eighty
7 90 ninety

8 1 18 degrees
2 27 degrees
3 4 degrees
4 28 degrees
5 11 degrees
6 36 degrees
7 13 degrees
8 40 degrees

Work skills p.19

2 1 It's eight o'clock.
2 It's one thirty.
3 It's four forty-five.
4 It's five fifteen.
5 It's nine o'clock.

4 1 10.00
2 11.00
3 1.45
4 3.45
5 5.00

Functions pp.20–21

2 ~~Scientist~~ Project manager
~~Salzburg~~ Lagos

3 1 Austria
2 Watertime Research
3 project manager
4 Nigeria

Focus
b job
c city
d company
e company
f country
g country

4 2 d   3 b   4 c   5 g   6 f   7 a

5 1 live in
2 travel to
3 work for
4 It's
5 I'm
6 work in

Review

Grammar pp.22–23

1 2 She isn't / She's not a doctor.
3 I'm not an architect.
4 They aren't / They're not from the United States.
5 ~~We aren't / We're not married.~~

2 2 Are they engineers?
3 Are you from the USA?
4 Is she married?
a 4   b 2   d 3

3 2 a   3 –   4 a   5 an   6 –

Vocabulary p.24

1 1 18
2 71
3 66
4 50
5 31
6 14

2 2 sixteen
3 eighty
4 fifteen
5 thirty-nine
6 sixty-six
7 thirty-one
8 eighteen

Work skills p.24

1 2 6:30
3 6:40
4 6:45
5 6:20
6 6:15
7 6:50

3 1 10.40   2 11.15   3 1.00   4 4.00

Functions p.25

1 1 Japan
2 Swords, Ireland
3 Adecco
4 America and Japan

2 Satoko is from Japan. She lives in Swords. It is in Ireland. She works for Adecco. It's a recruitment company. She's a recruitment officer. She travels to America and Japan.

3 1 Germany
2 Zurich, Switzerland
3 Credit Suisse
4 accounts manager
5 France and the UK

4 Andreas is from Germany. He lives in Zurich. It is in Switzerland. He works for Credit Suisse. It's a finance company. He's an accounts manager. He travels to France and the UK.

3

Grammar pp.26–27

2 1 an office rental company
2 New York
3 the UK

3 reception B   meeting room A   offices C   kitchen D
1 c   2 d   3 b   4 a   5 g   6 e   7 h   8 f

4 reception ✓   meeting room ✓   offices ✓   elevator ✓
parking ✓   internet connection ✓   kitchen ✓   shops ✓
restaurants ✓   train station ✓

5 1 False   2 False   3 True   4 True   5 False
6 True   7 False   8 True

Focus
We use *there* + **is** with singular nouns and *there* + **are** with plural nouns.
We use **Is** or **Are** + *there* to make a question.
We use *there* + **isn't** or **aren't** to make a negative sentence.

6 1 are
2 Are there
3 There's
4 is there
5 there's
6 is there
7 there is
8 Are there
9 there are
10 there's
11 Are there
12 there aren't

Vocabulary p.28

2 Post-its ✓   pencils ✓
a keyboard ✓   pens ✓
a mouse ✓   a computer ✓
a telephone ✓   paperclips
paper   a drawer ✓
a diary ✓

Work skills p.29

1 A – D   C – B

2 1 yes   3 yes
2 no   4 no

3 Emails B and C:
1 Hi   2 Agenda attached.   3 Bye
Emails A and D:
4 Mr Hussein   5 Ms Gonzales
6 Is 11.00 a.m. convenient for you?

Functions pp.30–31

2 Mona – espresso
Kim – cheese sandwich
Note – orange juice

3 1 Would   7 I'd
2 What   8 sandwich
3 espresso   9 What
4 espresso   10 like
5 Would   11 orange
6 What   12 please

Focus

Offering	Replying
Would you like something to drink /eat? *What would you like?*	*Yes, please.* No, thanks. I'd like a coffee, please. An orange juice, please.

Review

Grammar pp.32–33

1

/s/	/z/	/ɪz/
toilets	rooms	offices
banks	centres	bosses
car parks	managers	conferences

2 1 Is there a restaurant? Yes, there is.
2 There are eight meeting rooms.
3 There aren't any offices at the moment.
4 There is a conference room.
5 There isn't a car park.
6 Are there any banks? No, there aren't.

3 1 There's   5 there's
2 There are   6 Are there
3 there are   7 there's
4 Is there   8 Are there

4 1 Yes, there is.   4 Yes, there are.
2 No, there isn't.   5 No, there aren't.
3 Yes, there is.

Vocabulary p.34

1 desk   6 chair
2 pencil   7 keyboard
3 Post-its   8 stapler
4 books   9 paperclip
5 diary   10 mouse

Work skills p.34

1 Dear Mr Shaw
With best wishes / Best regards
2 Hi Catherine / Hi
Bye

Functions p.35

1 a ✓
b ✓
f ✓

2 1 Would you like   4 Would you like
2 What would you like?   5 I'd like
3 I'd like

3 1 a   2 a   3 a   4 b

Grammar pp.36–37

2 credit cards ✓   documents ✓
a mobile phone ✓   business cards ✓
a passport ✓   a laptop ✓
money ✓

3 1 Have   5 Yes
2 got   6 haven't
3 Has   7 No
4 hasn't   8 they've

Focus

To make positive sentences, we use *I/you/we/they* + **have** + *got*, or *he/she/it* + **has** + *got*.
To make questions, we use **Have** + *I/you/we/they* + *got*, or **Has** + *he/she/it* + *got*.
To make negative sentences and answers, we use **have** + *n't got*, or **has** + *n't got*.

4 2 Has Ella got her laptop?
3 Has Becky got the plane tickets?
4 Have they got the business cards?
5 Has Ella got the documents?
6 Have they got a gift?
7 Has Ella got a mobile phone?

Vocabulary p.38

1 M**on**day **Tues**day **Thurs**day **Fri**day **Sun**day

3 The weekend is **Saturday** and **Sunday**.

4 1 February   4 July
2 April   5 October
3 May   6 December

7 2 Monday, the eighth of February / Monday, February the eighth
3 Tuesday, the fifteenth of June / Tuesday, June the fifteenth
4 Thursday, the twenty-sixth of August / Thursday, August the twenty-sixth
5 Friday, the second of April / Friday, April the second
6 Saturday, the eleventh of September / Saturday, September the eleventh
7 Sunday, the sixteenth of May / Sunday, May the sixteenth
8 Wednesday, the third of November / Wednesday, November the third

8 15 October   19 October
23 October   30 October

Work skills p.39

1   1 How   4 speaking
    2 Could   5 calling
    3 It's

2   1 False   4 True
    2 True   5 False
    3 True

Functions pp.40–41

1   2 Wednesday   4 two o'clock
    3 2nd July   5 Jacques' office

2
Jacques	Hello, is that Karla? It's Jacques Brennard here.	1
Jacques	Thanks! Bye.	9
Jacques	Are you free on Wednesday morning for a meeting?	3
Jacques	Yes, the afternoon is OK. How about two o'clock?	5
Karla	OK. See you then.	8
Karla	Hi, Jacques. How can I help you?	2
Karla	Let me check … I'm sorry, I'm busy on Wednesday morning. How about in the afternoon?	4
Jacques	Great. So my office on Wednesday at two o'clock.	7
Karla	Yes, two o'clock is fine with me.	6

Focus

We use **Are you free …?** or **How about …?** to ask about the day and time.
We use **… is fine with me.** or **… is OK.** when we are free.
We use **I'm sorry. I'm busy.** when we are not free.

in – the morning, the afternoon
on – Monday, Tuesday afternoon
at – six o'clock, seven thirty

4   1 on   6 fine with
    2 in   7 OK
    3 on   8 about
    4 at   9 on
    5 at, on   10 at

Review

Grammar pp.42–43

1   1 have   5 s
    2 any   6 got
    3 haven't   7 have
    4 ve   8 any

2   2 Youssef has got a coffee cup.
    3 They haven't got any desk lights.
    4 Anna has got a printer.
    5 They haven't got two plane tickets.

3   2 Has   5 Has
    3 Has   6 Have
    4 Have

4   2 e   3 d   4 a   5 c   6 f

Vocabulary p.44

1   2 Wednesday   5 Thursday
    3 Monday   6 Sunday
    4 Saturday   7 Tuesday

2   Monday 4th April
    Tuesday 12th April
    Thursday 21st April

3   1 Saturday 30th April
    2 Monday 18th and Tuesday 19th April

4
o	oO	Oo	Oooo	oOo
March May June	*July*	April August	*January* February	September October November December

5   1 2015   4 1904
    2 1915   5 2020
    3 2004   6 1920

Work skills p.44

1   1 help   6 hold
    2 speak to   7 speaking
    3 please   8 from
    4 take   9 How
    5 It's   10 about

Functions p.45

1
in	on	at
the morning	Saturday	twelve p.m.
September	1st March	6.00 p.m.
December	Wednesday	lunchtime
the afternoon	morning	
	Monday	
	Friday evening	

2   1 are you free   5 OK
    2 Let me check   6 How about
    3 I'm busy   7 Thursday
    4 How about

5

Grammar pp.46–47

2   1 False   5 True
    2 False   6 False
    3 True   7 True
    4 True   8 False

Focus

Positive *he/she/it* verbs end in an **-s**.
To make questions, we use *Do + I/you/we/they* and **Does** + *he/she/it*.
To make the negative, we use *don't* and **doesn't**.

0%	50%	100%
never	sometimes	always

3   1 lives   4 gets up
    2 works   5 eats
    3 goes   6 speaks

5   1 Does Egil come from Brazil?
    2 Does he live in Rio de Janeiro?
    3 Is the Petrobras main office in São Paulo?
    4 Does he get up at 6.00?
    5 Does he get home at 9.30?
    6 Does he eat lunch in the office?
    7 Does he eat Norwegian food?
    8 Does he speak Portuguese?

6   1 No, he doesn't. He comes from Norway.
    2 No, he doesn't. He lives in São Paulo.
    3 No, it isn't. It's in Rio de Janeiro.
    4 Yes, he does.
    5 No, he doesn't. He gets home at 9.00.
    6 No, he doesn't. He eats lunch at one of the local restaurants.
    7 No, he doesn't. He never eats Norwegian food.
    8 Yes, he does.

7
1 get up
2 drink
3 take
4 work
5 eat
6 speak

Vocabulary p.48

1 1 a 2 f 3 g 4 e 5 d
6 c 7 b 8 h

2 2 by bus
3 by train
4 by bicycle
5 by taxi
6 on foot
7 by boat/ferry
8 by plane

5 1 Airport, gate
2 stand
3 pier
4 park
5 stop
6 platform

7 1 False
2 False
3 False
4 True
5 True
6 True

Work skills p.49

2 1 False
2 True
3 True
4 False

3 1 Elena Moretti
2 Milan
3 0039 85360001 extension 45
4 John (Davis)

4 He's/She's in a meeting at the moment / today.
He's/She's on another line at the moment.
He's/She's on a business trip at the moment / today / this week.
He's/She's out of the office at the moment / today / this week.
He's/She's on holiday at the moment / today / this week.
He's/She's not here at the moment / today / this week.

Functions pp.50–51

1 1 c 2 a 3 b

2

	likes	Lara's suggestions
Kenichi	walking	Holland Park
Wife	department stores	Harvey Nichols
Daughter	British culture	Victoria and Albert Museum

Focus
We use *like* + **noun** to talk about things we like.
We use *like* + **verb -ing** to talk about activities we like.
To make suggestions, we use *How about* + **verb -ing** or *Why don't you* + **verb**.

Review

Grammar pp.52–54

/s/	/z/
eats	lives
speaks	does
gets	buys

1 2 Does … live
3 goes
4 doesn't have
5 studies
6 Does … work
7 has
8 designs
9 doesn't speak
10 travels

2 1 uses
2 works
3 are
4 speak
5 speaks
6 talks
7 doesn't travel
8 enjoys

3 1 Does he; doesn't
2 Do we; do
3 Does she; doesn't
4 Does it; does

4 1 Do you work in an office?
2 Do you speak English at work?
3 Does your boss speak English?
4 Do you go to work by car?
5 Does your company have a website?
6 Do you go on business trips?
7 Do you get home late?

5 1 Yes, I do. / No, I don't.
2 Yes, I do. / No, I don't.
3 Yes, he/she does. / No, he/she doesn't.
4 Yes, I do. / No, I don't.
5 Yes, it does. / No, it doesn't.
6 Yes, I do. / No, I don't.
7 Yes, I do. / No, I don't.

Vocabulary p.54

1 1 Natalie
2 New York
3 bank
4 on foot
5 15 minutes
6 Marc
7 Paris
8 design
9 train
10 1 hour

2 1 airport, gate
2 pier
3 stop, station
4 stand
5 park
6 station, platform

Work skills pp.54–55

1 1 help
2 sorry
3 take
4 name
5 spell
6 number

2 1 1 Hording 2 Richmond 3 0470 3332145
2 1 Alisha 2 Olbrich 3 Brazil
4 0055 27 67590, extension 3 5 Ginny

Functions p.55

1 Example answers
I like walking.
I like music / going to concerts.
I like shopping.
I like art.
I like sightseeing.

2 1 I do
2 Why don't you
3 I don't
4 going
5 don't you
6 walking
7 about
8 Do you like
9 getting

6

Grammar pp.56–57

2 1 True
2 False
3 True
4 True
5 False
6 True
7 False

Focus

Subject pronouns	I	you	**he**	she	it	**we**	**they**
Object pronouns	**me**	you	him	**her**	it	us	**them**
Possessive adjectives	my	**your**	his	her	**its**	**our**	their

Subject pronouns come **before** the verb.
Object pronouns come **after** the verb.
Possessive adjectives come **before** nouns.

3 1 me
2 it
3 them
4 them
5 it

4 1 you; I
2 you; we
3 your; We
4 your; it
5 you, your; we, its, our
6 his, your; he, them
7 She, her
8 you, your; It, us

Vocabulary p.58

1 1 r 2 j 3 o 4 k 5 d 6 m 7 n
8 g 9 f 10 l 11 a 12 p 13 i 14 b
15 c 16 q 17 e 18 h

Work skills p.59

1 1 f 2 e 3 d 4 a 5 g 6 h 7 c
8 b

4 1 Costa
2 Paris
3 3,000 dirham
4 40–70 euros
5 40 euros
6 170 euros
7 free
8 2

Functions pp.60–61

2 1 Bocca di Leone
2 Helen Moran
3 7.30
4 two

4

	Soup	Salad	Pasta	Pizza	Water	Orange juice
Helen		✓	✓			✓
Silvio	✓			✓	✓	

5 1 OK
2 delicious
3 pretty good
4 really good
5 really good

Focus

We use *I'd like + to* + **verb** to say what we want to do.
We use *I'll **have*** + (food/drink) to order from a menu.

OK   pretty good   really good   delicious

6 A Certainly. For how many people?   3
B Yes, it's Kate Osbourne. O-S-B-O-U-R-N-E.   8
B Eight o'clock this evening.   6
A How can I help you?   1
A Thank you very much, Ms Osbourne. We'll see you at 8.00.   9
B I'd like to make a reservation, please.   2
B For eight.   4
B Thank you.   10
A Eight o'clock. And your name, please?   7
A For eight people. And from what time?   5

7 1 Waiter
2 Guests
3 Waiter
4 Guests
5 Guests
6 Waiter
7 Waiter
8 Guests

8 1 f 2 a 3 e 4 c 5 d 6 h 7 g
8 b

Review

Grammar pp.62–63

1 1 b 2 d 3 e 4 f 5 c 6 a

2 1 him
2 It's, its
3 You're, your
4 his, he's
5 me, your

3 1 them
2 he
3 He
4 they
5 They
6 She
7 She
8 We

4 1 Our
2 We
3 Our
4 his
5 Our
6 their

5 1 your
2 her
3 their
4 our
5 his

Vocabulary p.64

1 1 prawns
2 crab
3 aubergine
4 onion
5 chicken
6 beef
7 crisps
8 nuts
9 eggs
10 cheese

2 1 False
2 False
3 False
4 False
5 True
6 False
7 True
8 False

Work skills pp.64–65

1 48
2 120
3 570 euros
4 180 euros
5 26 euros
6 free
7 8
8 12 euros
9 1.2

Functions p.65

1 1 c 2 g 3 d 4 a 5 f 6 b 7 h
8 e

2

Making a reservation	1c
Ordering food and drink	3d, 7h
Asking about the food and meal	4a, 6b
Paying	5f, 8e

7

Grammar pp.66–67

2 1 True
2 False
3 False
4 True
5 False
6 True
7 True

Focus

Information	Question word
general facts	what, which
times or dates	when
people	who
places	where
numbers	how many

To make *Wh-* questions with *be*, we use *Wh-* + *be* + **subject**.
To make *Wh-* questions with *do*, we use *Wh-* + *do* + subject + **verb**.

3 1 What kind of company does Shirin work for?
2 Where is the main office?
3 What does Shirin do?
4 Where does she fly?
5 How many times does she fly in a month?
6 When does she have a break?
7 Who does she work with? / How many crew does she work with?

5 1 Which
2 What
3 Where
4 How many
5 Who
6 When

Vocabulary p.68

1
monorail	m	toilets	d	newsagent's	k
departures	a	security	f	baggage claim	h
information desk	j	taxi stand	n	bookshop	l
shops	e	restaurants	c	trolleys	i
parking	o	arrivals	g	check-in desks	b

3 1 l (bookshop) 2 j (information desk) 3 b (check-in desks)
4 k (newsagent's)

Work skills p.69

1 b

2 1 I'm writing to give you more information about your trip to Japan.
2 Please find the flight details attached.
3 Could you confirm these dates are OK as soon as possible?
4 And could I have your passport number so that I can book the flights?
5 Thank you for your email.
6 These dates are fine with me.
7 My passport number is 456 098 762 1.

3 A Dear Andrea
I am writing about a change in the dates for your trip to Japan. The outbound flight is Wednesday 18 November. The inbound flight is Thursday 26 November.
Could you confirm these dates are OK as soon as possible? And could I have the name of your hotel in Tokyo?
Best wishes
Momoko
B Dear Momoko
Thank you for your email. The new dates are fine with me.
My hotel is the Park Hyatt, Shinjuku.
Best wishes
Andrea

Functions pp.70–71

1 1 g 2 c 3 e 4 h 5 d 6 a 7 b
8 f

3 Cabin attendant: 1, 4, 6, 8 Passenger: 2, 3, 5, 7

4 1 c 2 a 3 b 4 e 5 d

Focus

The speaker wants X	The speaker wants the listener to do X
Could I have the pasta, please?	Could you close your window blind, please?
Have you got any more in-flight magazines?	Could you put your bag in the overhead locker?

We use **Could you** to ask someone to do something.
We use **Could I have** or **Have you got** to ask for something.
We use **Sure**, **OK** and **Certainly** to give a **positive** answer.

5 1 Could I 3 Could I 5 Have you got
2 Could you 4 Could you 6 Could you

Review

Grammar pp.72–73

1 Who 3 Where 5 What
2 When 4 How many 6 How many

2 1 What does she study?
2 Where do they work?
3 When do you start work?
4 What time do you finish work?
5 Who does she work for?
6 When does the train arrive?
7 What time does it leave?
8 What do they want?
9 When is your birthday?
10 Where is Barcelona?

3 Example answers
1 I work for ATT.
2 I'm based in Japan.
3 I've got an engineering degree.
4 250 people work for my company.
5 I speak three languages.
6 I start work at 8.00.
7 I finish work at 5.00.
8 I go to three conferences a year.

4
Sally	Hi, I'm Sally.	1
Jaime	I work for Logun Ltd.	4
Sally	Where is Bordeaux?	7
Sally	Ah yes. Is Bordeaux big? How many people live there?	9
Sally	Nice to meet you too. Who do you work for, Jaime?	3
Sally	I live in Birmingham, in the UK.	11
Jaime	About 100,000. What about you, Sally? Where do you live?	10
Sally	Oh, and where is Logun Ltd based?	5
Jaime	In Bordeaux.	6
Jaime	It's in France.	8
Jaime	Hi, I'm Jaime. Nice to meet you.	2

5 1 e 2 c 3 g 4 d 5 a 6 b 7 f
She's a hotel inspector.

Vocabulary p.74

1 toilets 6 security
2 monorail 7 departures
3 bookshop 8 parking
4 newsagent's 9 arrivals
5 trolleys 10 check-in desks

Work skills p.74

2 1 I'm writing to give you more information
2 find the details
3 confirm
4 could I
5 taxi

Functions p.75

1 Could I 6 Could
2 here you are 7 here
3 Could you 8 Could you
4 Sure / Certainly / OK 9 Could you
5 Could I 10 of

8

Grammar pp.76–77

1 1 b 2 c 3 d 4 a

2 The Beatles, Fred Astaire, Frank Sinatra

3 1 True 4 True
2 True 5 False
3 False

4 1 Yes, it did. 5 2007
2 Yes, they did. 6 220
3 four husbands 7 2010
4 No, she didn't.

Focus

To make the Past Simple for regular verbs, we add **-ed** to the end of the verb.
To make the Past Simple of *be*, we use *I / you / we / they were* and *he / she / it* **was**.

To make a question in the Past Simple, we use **Did** + subject + verb.
To make positive short answers, we use **did**.
To make negative short answers, we use **didn't**.
To make a *Wh-* question in the Past Simple, we use *Wh-* + **did** + subject + verb.

5
1 opened
2 stayed
3 painted
4 lived
5 danced
6 played
7 visited
8 was, were

7
1 opened
2 painted
3 lived
4 did
5 danced
6 played
7 No, didn't

9
1 opened
2 was
3 created
4 managed
5 introduced
6 stayed
7 lived
8 used

Vocabulary p.78

1 1 h 2 d 3 a 4 c
5 f 6 e 7 b 8 g

3
1 reservation
2 reception
3 registration form, passport, credit card
4 key card
5 lift
6 bags

4 1 b 2 d 3 a 4 c 5 e 6 f 7 g 8 i 9 j 10 h

6 open: window, wardrobe
have: bath, shower
turn on: television, shower, light

Work skills p.79

1
1 Millena Scot
2 two
3 single
4 500 euros

2 Dear Ms **Scott**
Here is confirmation of your booking:

Guest name	**Milena Scott**
Confirmation number	**89917**
Arrival date	**Sunday 14th** August
Departure date	Wednesday 17th August
Room type	Standard **double**
Room rate per night	**315** euros

3
1 have
2 repeat
3 two
4 correct
5 350
6 315
7 say that again

Functions pp.80–81

1 1 c 2 e 3 g 4 f 5 h 6 b 7 a
8 d

4
1 True
2 False
3 True
4 True
5 False

Focus

Checking in	Checking out
I'd like to check in.	Have you got your key card?
Have you got any bags?	Here's your bill.
Would you like the porter to take it to your room?	Here's your receipt.
Is there a lift?	Can you please check the amount and enter your pin?
Here is your key card.	I'd like to check out, please.
You are in room 306.	How would you like to pay?

5
1 Dr Ziegert
2 one
3 single
4 204
5 second

Review

Grammar pp.82–83

1
1 It was a luxury hotel.
2 She was a celebrity.
3 There were four lifts.
4 The guests were famous.
5 He lived in Jamaica.
6 It closed in 2010.

2

/d/	/t/	/ɪd/
lived	danced	started
stayed	worked	painted
filmed	finished	invented
opened		
played		
moved		

3
1 they did
2 he didn't
3 he did
4 she did
5 she didn't

4
1 opened
2 developed, added
3 created
4 stayed
5 started

Vocabulary pp.83–84

1 1 c 2 e 3 d 4 a 5 g 6 b 7 f

2
1 bed
2 bathroom, bath, shower
3 wardrobe, window, door
4 television, light, shower
5 television
6 towel

3
1 credit card
2 shower
3 key card
4 passport
5 towel
6 light

Work skills p.84

1 name
2 repeat
3 Richard Deccard
4 'c'
5 2nd October
6 How much
7 two
8 30th September
9 2nd October
10 double
11 240
12 say that

Functions p.85

1
1 check in
2 spell
3 nights
4 fill
5 passport
6 credit card
7 key
8 are
9 floor
10 bags
11 porter

2
A Good morning. I'd like to check out, please. Room 222. 1
B How would you like to pay? 6
B Thank you. Room 222 … One moment please, sir. … Here's your bill. Would you like to check it? 4
A Yes, here it is. 3
B Of course. No problem. Have you got your key card, sir? 2
B Thank you. Here's your receipt. Have a nice day. Goodbye. 8
A Yes, please. … It's fine. 5
A Goodbye. 9
A Cash. 7

9

Grammar pp.86–87

1 1 February 2010
2 France
3 yes
4 He got very sick.
5 He met his friends in Brisbane.
6 no
7 No, because it doesn't have any roads.
8 on 1st August

Focus

To form a question in the Past Simple with *be*, we use *was/were* + **subject** + adjective.
To form the negative in the Past Simple with *be*, we use **wasn't** and *weren't*.

2 1 made
2 ate
3 slept
4 took
5 took
6 rode
7 saw, had
8 was
9 did
10 made

3 1 went
2 had
3 got
4 made
5 ate
6 took
7 began
8 rose
9 slept
10 came

Vocabulary p.88

1 2 post office
3 clothes shop / department store
4 station
5 cinema
6 museum
7 café
8 bank

2 2 b   3 d   4 a   5 e

3 1 library   2 hotel   3 supermarket   4 bookshop

4 1 Ocean, between
2 Park, next
3 corner, Park, opposite

Work skills p.89

1 1 b   2 g   3 d   4 h   5 a   6 e   7 f
8 c

3 1 Tata Motors
2 It was quite long, but the service was very good.
3 near the office
4 yes
5 yes
6 in the main meeting room

Functions pp.90–91

1 2 f   3 g   4 b   5 a   6 d   7 c

2 1 Italian restaurant   3 Chinese restaurant
2 post office

Focus

Asking for directions	Giving the location	Giving directions
Where is the Grand Hotel? Is there a bank near here? How do I get to the hospital?	*It's on Elm Way.* It's at the end of Station Hill Road. The hotel is next to the bank. The restaurant is on the left.	Go straight on. Turn left at the cinema. Turn right at the coffee shop.

3 1 1 down
2 right
3 Park Street
4 left
5 shoe

2 1 end
2 down
3 past
4 left

3 1 left
2 end
3 left

Review

Grammar pp.92–93

1 1 bought
2 come
3 Was
4 sell
5 spoke
6 win
7 have
8 buy
9 was
10 Was

3 Example answers
I bought / didn't buy a newspaper.
I went / didn't go on a business trip.
I spoke / didn't speak to my boss.
I went / didn't go to a restaurant.
I saw / didn't see an old friend.
I began / didn't begin a new project.

Vocabulary pp.93–94

1 1 c   2 a   3 e   4 b   5 d

2 In picture A, the café is next to the supermarket. In picture B, the bank is next to the supermarket.
In picture A, the bus stop is opposite the supermarket. In picture B, a taxi is opposite the supermarket.
In picture A, a bank is between the hotel and the chemist's. In picture B, a restaurant is between the hotel and the chemist's.
In picture A, two men and a woman are sitting on the bench. In picture B, a man and two women are sitting on the bench.

Work skills p.94

1 1 Pleased to meet you.
2 How was your flight this morning?
3 How is the hotel?
4 Would you like a drink?
5 Can I help you with anything else?
6 Please come this way.

2 1 Mr Henri
2 b
3 yes
4 No, it's very quiet.
5 a mineral water

Functions p.95

1 1 c   2 a   3 b

2 1 Excuse
2 Where's
3 Queen's Road
4 How
5 turn
6 turn right
7 left
8 opposite

10

Grammar pp.96–97

1 1 book
2 fly
3 email
4 meet
5 send
6 call
7 arrange
8 invite
9 ask
10 get
11 buy
12 learn

2 1 Hong Kong
2 meet Kay at the airport
3 arrange a meeting with DesignHK
4 design some of their new products
5 everyone from DesignHK

Focus

To form the *going to* future, we use *be + going to* + **verb**.
We use *going to* to talk about intentions and **plans** for the future.

3 1 She's going to book her flight to Hong Kong.
2 She's going to send Yiyi Chen the flight details.
3 She's going to call Joseph Nolan.
4 She's going to ask him for suggestions about restaurants.
5 She's going to get some Hong Kong dollars from the bank.
6 She's going to buy some summer clothes.
7 She's going to learn ten new phrases in Chinese.

4 1 am
2 are
3 meet
4 are
5 visit
6 stay
7 do
8 go
9 we are
10 have
11 fly

Vocabulary p.98

1 1 j 2 i 3 f 4 c 5 d 6 e 7 g
8 h 9 a 10 b

2 1 Spanish
2 German
3 Swedish
4 Japanese
5 Korean
6 Italian
7 American
8 French
9 British
10 Swiss

3 See script 10.3.

Work skills p.99

2 1 DesignHK asked for an extra 10%.
2 yes
3 no
4 They're really great.

3 a 3 b 1 c 2, 4, 5

5 a 2, 5 b 4 c 1 d 3

Functions pp.100–101

2 1 Antonia, Maia
2 Claire, Ian
3 Claudia, Mario
4 Joseph, Kay

Focus

Thanking someone	Thank you very much for coming. Thanks for everything.
Wishing someone a good trip home	Have a good flight. I hope you have a safe journey.
Saying you enjoyed meeting	It was lovely to meet you. It was nice to see you again. It was great working together.
Talking about future contact	I'll be in touch again. I look forward to it / working with you again. See you again next month. I'll call you next week.
Saying goodbye	Bye. Goodbye. Bye for now.

3 1 a 3 b 1 c 4 d 2
2 a 2 b 5 c 3 d 1 e 6 f 4
3 a 4 b 2 c 5 d 1 e 3

Grammar p.102

1 2 She's going to **fly Cathay Pacific**.
3 Yiyi and Kay **are** going to meet at the **airport**.
4 **Kay's** going to invite everyone from DesignHK for **dinner**.
5 Kay and Doctor Wu **are** going to have **dinner** together.
6 Kay is going to **buy** some new **clothes**.
7 She**'s** going to get some money at the **bank**.
8 She's going to **learn ten** phrases in **Chinese**.

2 1 e 2 f 3 b 4 a 5 g 6 d 7 c

3 I'm going to check the map.
I'm going to practise the interview with a friend.
I'm going to finish my presentation.
I'm going to buy a new suit.
I'm going to look at the company website.
I'm going to write a new CV.

Vocabulary pp.103–104

1 1 Saudi Arabian
2 Brazilian
3 French
4 Russian
5 Japanese
6 Italian
7 British
8 Chinese
9 Spanish
10 Argentinian
11 Dutch
12 American

3

Airline	Country	Nationality
1 Virgin Airlines	Britain	**British**
2 Delta	**the USA**	American
3 JAL	Japan	**Japanese**
4 Lufthansa	**Germany**	German
5 Qantas	Australia	**Australian**
6 Thai Airways	**Thailand**	Thai

4 Delta is an American company.
JAL is a Japanese company.
Lufthansa is a German company.
Qantas is an Australian company.
Thai Airways is a Thai company.

5 1 the USA
2 Brazil
3 Argentina
4 Britain
5 Spain
6 France
7 Holland
8 Germany
9 Switzerland
10 Italy
11 Sweden
12 Russia
13 Saudi Arabia
14 South Korea
15 Japan
16 China
17 Thailand
18 Australia

Work skills p.104

1 1 I've got
2 think
3 good news
4 attached
5 like
6 call

2 1 sorry to hear
2 Do you mean
3 I think
4 pleased
5 call

Functions p.105

Ms Oxendon	I will. See you next summer!	5
Ms Oxendon	Please say thank you to Karl from me.	4
Ms Sasaki	Goodbye.	7
Ms Oxendon	You're welcome.	3
Ms Sasaki	Thank you. And thank you for everything.	2
Ms Sasaki	Goodbye.	6
Ms Oxendon	Goodbye Shiho. I hope you have a safe journey home.	1

3 1 a 2 b 3 b 4 b

INTERNATIONAL EXPRESS

EXPRESS

BEGINNER

Pocket Book

Contents

Pocket Book Guide

Here is some information about the Pocket Book.

1 There are short examples of conversations for each section of the Student's Book. You can listen to these conversations using the audio files. The audio is on the DVD-ROM in your Student's Book Pack. Here are some suggestions.

  1 You can practise your listening. Just play the audio and listen. Listen a little bit every day to improve your listening skills.

  2 You can practise your speaking. You can take the **B** part and answer **A** in each conversation.

  3 You can practise your pronunciation. Listen carefully to how the people speak. Copy their pronunciation.

  4 You can improve your memory. Cover the **B** line. Then read the **A** line. Repeat until you can remember the **B** line.

2 You can check the notes in the Student's Book for each language point. The reference page is at the end of each section.

3 You can add your own translation of the vocabulary. Ask your teacher to help you or use a dictionary.

4 You can use the *Classroom language* section in class. Keep your Pocket Book on your desk and check the right phrase to use to ask questions, check meaning, and so on.

5 You can use the *Coursebook language* section to help you understand the important study words like *correct*, *match*, and *practise*. The *Grammar words* section gives you some more study words about grammar.

6 The *Irregular verbs* section gives you a reference for common irregular verbs in the Present Simple and Past Simple. It also helps you with Unit 9 in the Student's Book.

7 Take the Pocket Book with you to work. Keep it on your desk. Practise when you have spare time. Use it when you make a phone call or before you meet someone.

8 Take the Pocket Book on business trips or on holiday. Use the phrases, for example, from Unit 6 *Eating out* or Unit 8 *Checking in and out of a hotel*.

Grammar

UNIT **1** *be: I, you, he, she, it, we, they*

1 A Hello, I*'m* Fábio da Costa.
  B Hi, I*'m* Li Zhang.

2 A You*'re* from China. Is that right?
  B Yes, I*'m* from Shanghai.

3 A Maria *is* from Brazil.
  B Yes, she*'s* from Recife.

4 A Ottawa *is* in the United States.
  B No, it*'s* in Canada.

5 A Hi, I*'m* Maria and this *is* Jean.
  B Hello. I*'m* Tim. I*'m* from the UK.
  A We*'re* from Senegal.

6 A Mahmoud and Aziz *are* from Dubai.
  B Dubai? I think they*'re* from Saudi Arabia.

Reference: Student's Book **p.12**

UNIT **2** *be: questions and negatives*

1 A *Are you* from Japan?
  B Yes, I am. I'm from Nagoya.

2 A *Are you* from France?
  B No, *I'm not*. I'm from Spain.

3 A He's a scientist.
  B No, he *isn't* a scientist. He's a lawyer.

4 A *Is he* twenty seven?
  B Yes, he is.

5 A *Is* Trieste in France?
  B No, *it isn't*. It's in Italy.

6 A *Are you* and Elena from Spain?

  B Yes, we are. We're from Burgos.

7 A *Are they* from Saudi Arabia?

  B No, *they're not*. They're from Dubai.

Reference: Student's Book **p.22**

UNIT ▮3▮ *there is, there are*

1 A *Is there* a car park at the hotel?

  B Yes, *there is*. There's space for 400 cars.

2 A *Are there* five meeting rooms?

  B Yes, *there are*. There's also a large conference room.

3 A *Is there* a gym in the hotel?

  B No, *there isn't* a gym, but *there are* two swimming pools.

4 A *Is there* a train station near here?

  B No, *there isn't*. There's a bus station across the road.

5 A *Are there* any offices on the third floor?

  B No, *there aren't*. There's a restaurant on that floor.

6 A *Are there* any banks near the hotel?

  B Yes, *there are* two banks near the hotel.

7 A *Are there* any bars in the conference centre?

  B No, *there aren't* any bars, but there is an internet café.

Reference: Student's Book **p.32**

UNIT ▮4▮ *have got, has got*

1 A *Have you got* a mobile phone?

  B Yes, I have.

2 A *Has he got* the tickets?

  B Yes, he has.

3 A *Have you got* the documents?
   B No, I haven't.

4 A *Have you got* a book?
   B No, I *haven't got* a book. I've got a magazine.

5 A *Has he got* a laptop?
   B No, he *hasn't* got a laptop. He's *got* an iPad.

Reference: Student's Book **p.42**

UNIT 5 *he, she, it + verb; do, does*

1 A *Does he live* in Zurich?
   B Yes, *he does.*

2 A *Does he work* in Zurich?
   B No, *he works* in Lucerne.

3 A *Do you drive* to work?
   B Yes, I do.

4 A *Does he work* for a company?
   B No, *he doesn't.*

5 A *Do you live* in Madrid?
   B No, *I don't.* I live in Barcelona.

Reference: Student's Book **p.52**

UNIT 6 *I, me, my*

1 A Are *you* in Dubai now?
   B No, *I'm* in Abu Dhabi.

2 A Does Paulo like *his* new house?
   B Yes, *he* loves *it.*

3 A Does Mira talk to *her* friends?
   B Yes, *she* talks to *them* on the phone.

4 A Is this *your* bag?
   B No, I don't think so. *My* bag is in the car.

5 A Do you know Helen?
   B Yes, I met *her* in Cairo.

6 A Does Helen work with Paulo?
   B Yes, *she's* *his* boss.

7 A Do *your* friends live in Abu Dhabi?
   B Yes, *their* house is very near *our* house.

Reference: Student's Book **p.62**

UNIT 7 Questions: *Wh-* +, *How* +

1 A *Where* does he work?
   B He works in Dubai.

2 A *Where* is your office?
   B It's in the city centre.

3 A *What* do you do?
   B I'm an engineer.

4 A *When* is the next meeting?
   B It's tomorrow morning.

5 A *How many* people does she work with?
   B She works with three people.

6 A *What* kind of company do you work for?
   B I work for an airline company.

7 A *Who* does he work with?
   B He works with the cabin attendants.

Reference: Student's Book **p.72**

UNIT 8 Past Simple: *be*, regular verbs

1 A *Did* the hotel *open* last year?
   B Yes, it *did*.

2 A *When did* the Queen *stay* there?
   B She *stayed* there in 1957.

3 A *Did* the chef *create* a salad?
   B Yes, he *created* the Waldorf Salad.

4 A *Did* you *like* the hotel?
   B Yes, I *did*. It was amazing.

5 A *What did* you do yesterday?
   B I *watched* a film.

Reference: Student's Book **p.82**

UNIT 9 Past Simple: irregular verbs

1 A *Where did* you *go* on holiday?
   B I *went* to India.

2 A *When did* you *get* your passport?
   B I *got* it last week.

3 A *What did* you *take* with you?
   B I *took* a travel bag and some books.

4 A *Who did* you *have* lunch with?
   B I *had* lunch with my friend.

5 A *Did* you *sleep* well?
   B Yes, I *slept* very well, thanks.

6 A *Was* it fun?
   B Yes, it *was* great fun.

Reference: Student's Book **p.92**

1 A Your room isn't very tidy.

  B I know. I'm *going to tidy* it soon.

2 A Your bicycle is pretty dirty.

  B I know. I'm *going to clean* it tomorrow.

3 A You owe me £5 pounds.

  B I know. I'm *going to give* it to you soon.

4 A Your mum called yesterday.

  B I know. I'm *going to call* her this evening.

5 A You don't have any ties.

  B I know. I'm *going to buy* some at the weekend.

Reference: Student's Book **p.102**

Vocabulary

UNITS **1** and **2** Numbers

1	one	30	thirty
2	two	40	forty
3	three	50	fifty
4	four	60	sixty
5	five	70	seventy
6	six	80	eighty
7	seven	90	ninety
8	eight	100	a hundred
9	nine		
10	ten	31	thirty-one
11	eleven	32	thirty-two
12	twelve	33	thirty-three
13	thirteen	34	thirty-four
14	fourteen	35	thirty-five
15	fifteen	36	thirty-six
16	sixteen	37	thirty-seven
17	seventeen	38	thirty-eight
18	eighteen	39	thirty-nine
19	nineteen		
20	twenty		

UNIT **3** My workstation

Word	Translation
books	
chair	
computer	
desk	
diary	

drawer	
mouse	
paperclips	
pencils	
pens	
post-its	
paper	
telephone	

UNIT **4** Days, months, and dates

Monday	January	July
Tuesday	February	August
Wednesday	March	September
Thursday	April	October
Friday	May	November
Saturday	June	December
Sunday		

first	eleventh	twenty-first
second	twelfth	twenty-second
third	thirteenth	twenty-third
fourth	fourteenth	twenty-fourth
fifth	fifteenth	twenty-fifth
sixth	sixteenth	twenty-sixth
seventh	seventeenth	twenty-seventh
eighth	eighteenth	twenty-eighth
ninth	nineteenth	twenty-ninth
tenth	twentieth	thirtieth
		thirty-first

1st January	the first of January, January the first
2nd February	the second of February, February the second
3rd March	the third of March, March the third

2001	two thousand and one
2012	twenty twelve
2015	twenty fifteen
2020	twenty twenty

UNIT 5 Getting around

Word	Translation
car	
train	
bicycle / bike	
bus	
plane	
boat	
ferry	
taxi	
terminal	
platform	
bus stop	
pier	
airport	
gate	

UNIT 6 Food and drink

Word	Translation
chips / French fries	
burger	
pasta	
pizza	

soup	
salad	
rice	
noodles	
kebabs	
couscous	
chicken curry	
nan bread	
baguette	
croissant	
oranges	
bananas	
tiramisu	
ice cream	
prawns	
crab	
aubergine	
zucchini	
onion	
chicken	
beef	
crisps	
nuts	
eggs	
cheese	

UNIT 7 Airports

Word	Translation
monorail	
departures	
information desk	
shops	
parking	
toilets	
security	
taxi stand	
restaurants	
arrivals	
newsagent's	
baggage claim	
bookshop	
trolleys	
check-in desks	

UNIT 8 Hotels

Word	Translation
reception	
bags	
key card	
credit card	
registration form	
reservation	
passport	
lift / elevator	

bed	
television	
wardrobe	
window	
light	
bathroom	
bath	
shower	
towel	
door	

UNIT 9 Locations

Word	Translation
post office	
department store	
bank	
station	
cinema	
museum	
café	
pavement	
road	
corner	
traffic lights	
between	
next to	
opposite	
at the end	
on the corner	

Country	Nationality
Spain	Spanish
Germany	German
Sweden	Swedish
Japan	Japanese
South Korea	Korean
Italy	Italian
the USA	American
France	French
Britain	British
Switzerland	Swiss
Poland	Polish
Brazil	Brazilian
Greece	Greek
China	Chinese
Thailand	Thai
India	Indian
Holland	Dutch

Work skills

UNIT **1** Spelling

1 **A** Hi, my name's Jane Brookes.
   B Can you spell that, please?
   A Yes. Jane. J-A-N-E. Brookes. B-R-O-O-K-E-S.
   B B-R-O-O-K-E-S? Is that right?
   A Yes, that's right.

2 **A** Hi, I'm Kenji Watanabe.
   B Can you spell Watanabe, please?
   A Sure. W-A-T-A-N-A-B-E.
   B Thank you.

UNIT **2** Talking about schedules

1 The meeting is at one o'clock.
                      one fifteen.
                      one thirty.
                      one forty-five.

2 **A** Excuse me. What time is lunch?
   B At twelve thirty.
   A Thanks.

3 **A** Is the workshop at two o'clock?
   B Actually, it's at one forty-five.
   A One forty-five. OK, thanks.

4 **A** What time is it, please?
   B It's four fifteen.

5 **A** Is the coffee break at ten thirty?
   B Yes, that's right.

UNIT **4** Telephoning 1

1 A Could I speak to Jay Ashton, please?
   B Of course. One moment, please.

2 A Could I take your name, please?
   B Yes, it's Peter Fox.

3 A Jay Ashton, speaking.
   B Hi, Jay. It's Peter.
   A Oh, hi Peter. How are you?
   B Fine, thanks. I'm calling about your visit.

UNIT **5** Telephoning 2

1 A Could I speak to Sebastian Mila?
   B I'm sorry. He's not in the office just now. Can I take a message?
   A No, that's OK.

2 A Hi. Is that Lara?
   B No, this is Nicole. Lara's in a meeting.
   A Oh, hi Nicole. Could you ask Lara to call me?
   B Sure. Does she have your number?
   A No. It's 779015.

UNIT **6** Travelling and money

1 A Is Japan expensive?
   B Yes, it's quite expensive.

2 A How much is a hotel in Tokyo?
   B It's about 100 euros.

3 A Is the exchange rate good?
   B It's OK. 100 yen is about one euro.

4 A Is internet access good?
   B Yes, it's very fast.

UNIT 8 Giving and checking information

1 **A** Could I have your name, please?
  B Yes, it's Birgit Hoffmeister.
  A Could you repeat that, please?
  B Yes, it's Birgit Hoffmeister.
  A Is that Hoffmeister with two ff's?
  B Yes, that's right.

2 **A** How much is a double room?
  B It's two hundred and fifteen euros.
  A I'm sorry. Is that two hundred and fifty euros?
  B No, it's two hundred and fif*teen* euros.

UNIT 9 Looking after a visitor

1 **A** How was your flight?
  B It was very good, thanks.

2 **A** Would you like a drink?
  B Yes, I'll have some water, please.

3 **A** How is your hotel?
  B It's very comfortable.

4 **A** Shall we go through your schedule?
  B That's a good idea.

Functions

UNIT **1** Introductions and greetings

1 A Good afternoon. My name's Tim Brown and this is Jo Williams.
   B Good afternoon. My name's Irina Ivanova. Pleased to meet you both.

2 A Good morning. My name's Javier Gonzalez.
   B Pleased to meet you, Javier. I'm Li Qin.
   A Hello, Li Qin. Nice to meet you too.

3 A Hello. Welcome to the conference. Can I take your name?
   B Sure. My name's Ken Scott.

4 A Hello, I'm Adriana Gilberto.
   B I'm sorry?
   A My name is Adriana Gilberto.
   B Hello, Adriana. I'm Philippe Tournier.

5 A Excuse me, I'm Johanna Schneider.
   B Sorry, can you spell 'Schneider', please?
   A Of course, that's S-C-H-N-E-I-D-E-R.
   B Thank you.

6 A Good morning.
   B Morning.
   A How are you?
   B Fine thanks. And you?
   A I'm well, thanks.

Reference: Student's Book **p.14–15**

UNIT **2** Exchanging personal information

1 A Hello. My name is Jean Bouyer.
   B Hi, Jean. Pleased to meet you. I'm Mark Adams.

2 A Where are you from?

B I'm from Ireland. And you?
A I'm from the Czech Republic. I live in Brno.

3 A Are you from Argentina?
   B Yes, I am. I live in Buenos Aires.

4 A Where is your office?
   B I work in Moscow. My office is in the city centre.

5 A Are you an engineer?
   B Yes, I am. I work for a car company.

6 A So you live in Australia.
   B Yes, but I travel to Indonesia and Malaysia for my job.
   A Really? How interesting!
   B And you?
   A I work for TZP Electrics. It's a manufacturing company.
   B Really? Where is your headquarters?
   A It's in Guangzhou in China.

Reference: Student's Book **p.25**

UNIT **3** Offering and accepting food and drinks

1 A Would you like something to drink?
   B Yes, please.
   A What would you like?
   B A coffee, please.

2 A Would you like something to eat?
   B Yes. I'd like a tuna sandwich, please.
   A OK.

3 A What would you like to drink?
   B An orange juice, please.
   A I'm sorry. There isn't any orange juice. There's grapefruit.
   B OK. A grapefruit juice, please.

Reference: Student's Book **p.35**

UNIT **4** Making an arrangement

1 A Are you free on Tuesday afternoon?
B Let me check. Sorry, I'm busy then.

2 A Are you free this morning?
B I'm sorry. I'm busy. How about this afternoon?
A OK. How about three o'clock?
B That's fine.

3 A Are you free at four o'clock?
B I'm busy at four. How about five?
A Five is fine. See you then.

Reference: Student's Book **p.45**

UNIT **5** Talking about things you like; making suggestions

1 A Do you like shopping?
B Yes, I do.

2 A What do you like doing?
B I like visiting museums.

3 A Why don't you go to the British Museum?
B That's a good idea.

4 A How about having lunch in a Chinese restaurant?
B That's a great idea.

5 A Do you like Italian food?
B Yes, I do.
A How about having pizza for lunch?
B Great.

Reference: Student's Book **p.55**

UNIT 6 Eating out

1 **A** I'd like to make a reservation.
    B For how many people?
    A For four people.
    B Certainly.

2 **A** Are you ready to order?
    B Yes, I'd like the salad, please.

3 **A** What would you like for the main course?
    B I'll have the spaghetti pomodoro.

4 **A** How's your spaghetti?
    B It's delicious.

5 **A** How was your meal?
    B It was very good, thank you.

6 **A** Could we have the bill, please?
    B Certainly.

Reference: Student's Book **p.65**

UNIT 7 Making requests

1 **A** Could you return to your seat, please?
    B Yes, of course.

2 **A** Could I have a menu, please?
    B Certainly, sir.

3 **A** Have you got any more in-flight magazines?
    B I'll have a look for you, madam.

4 **A** Could I see your boarding card, please?
    B OK.

5 **A** Could you open your bag for me?
    B Sure.

Reference: Student's Book **p.75**

UNIT 8 Checking in and out of a hotel

1 A Can I help you?
  B Yes, I'd like to check in, please.

2 A Do you have your passport and credit card?
  B Yes, here they are.

3 A Would you like a twin or a double room?
  B A double, please.

4 A Have you got any bags?
  B Just this one.

5 A I'd like to check out, please.
  B OK. Have you got your key card?
  A Yes, here you are.

6 A Would you like to pay by credit card?
  B Yes.

7 A Can you check the amount and enter your pin number?
  B OK.

Reference: Student's Book **p.85**

UNIT 9 Asking for and giving directions

1 A Is there a park near here?
  B Yes, there's one at the end of this road on the left.

2 A Excuse me, where's the train station?
  B It's on this road. Go straight on. It's on the right.

3 A Is there a bookshop near here?
  B Yes, there's one on Ship Street. Take the first left and it's on your right.

4 A Excuse me, where's the museum?
  B It's on King Street. Go down this road. Turn right at the bookshop. It's on the right.

Reference: Student's Book **p.95**

UNIT 10 Saying *thank you* and *goodbye*

1 **A** It was great to see you. Thanks for your help.
  B My pleasure.
  A See you next month.
  B Look forward to it.

2 **A** Goodbye, Gemma. It was very nice to meet you.
  B I hope we meet again next year.
  A Me, too.

3 **A** Bye, Gino.
  B Bye, Toshiko. Have a safe journey.
  A Thanks. I'll call you.

Reference: Student's Book **p.105**

Classroom language

Here are some phrases to use in the classroom.

Phrase	Translation
Could you say that again?	
How do you spell 'internet'?	
What does 'reception' mean?	
How do you say 'autobus' in English?	
Sorry, I don't understand.	
What should I do?	
I don't know the answer to number 3.	
I've finished.	
Who is my partner?	
Sorry I'm late.	
I need to leave early.	

Here are some phrases to use for pair work.

Phrase	Translation
Are you ready?	
Let's start.	
Is it my turn?	
I think you're right.	
Are you sure?	
May be the answer is …	
What do you think?	
It's your turn.	
What's the answer?	
Let's ask the teacher.	
That's a good idea.	

Coursebook language

Here are some phrases from your Student's Book. You can add a translation in the box below the phrase.

Verb	Phrase
answer	Answer the questions in exercise 4.
ask	Ask your partner questions about their job.
check	Listen and check your answers.
choose	Choose the best answer to the questions.
circle	Listen and circle the numbers you hear.
complete	Complete the sentences.
conversation	Listen to the conversation.
correct	Correct the mistakes.
fill in	Fill in the gaps.
finish	Finish the conversation.
find	Read the sentences and find the places on the map.
introduce	Introduce yourself to three students in the class.
label	Label the pictures.
listen	Listen to the conversation.

Verb	Phrase
look at	Look at the picture.
match	Match the pictures with the labels.
order	Order the conversation.
practise	Practise the conversation in exercise 5 with a partner.
read	Read the conversation.
repeat	Listen and repeat the numbers.
role-play	Work in threes. Role-play this telephone conversation.
say	Say your name.
spell	Spell your name for your partner.
talk about	Listen to Yasmina talking about the food she eats.
talk to	Talk to your partner about the text.
tell	Tell the class about your partner.
tick	Listen and tick [✓] the correct answer.
underline	Underline the correct answer.
use	Complete the table. Use the phrases from the box.
work	Work with a partner.
write	Write the names of the countries.

Grammar words

Here are some grammar words to help you with your studying.

Word	Definition
adjective	a word that describes a person or a thing **Example** This drink is *hot*.
adverb	a word that tells you how, when, or where something happens **Example** Please speak *slowly*.
article	*a* or *an* are indefinite articles, and *the* is the definite article **Example** There is *a* computer on *the* table.
noun	a word that you use for a person, place, thing, or idea **Example** My *company* has an *office* in *Munich*.
plural	more than one person or thing: **Example** He has got two *jobs*.
possessive adjective	the form of a word that shows that something belongs to someone **Example** It's *your* notebook.
preposition	a word that tells you where, when, how, etc. **Example** He is travelling *from* London *to* Paris *on* 5th March.
pronoun	a word that you use in place of a noun **Example** *She* gave *it* to *you*.
singular	the form of a word that shows there is only one person or thing **Example** There's one *man* in the meeting room.
verb	a word that tells you what somebody does or what happens **Example** She *lives* in Windsor and *works* in London.

Irregular verbs

Here are some common irregular verbs.

be	*am*, *is*, *are*	*was*, *were*
	I *am* a project manager.	I *was* a project manager.
	He *is* a student.	He *was* a student.
	They *are* tired.	They *were* tired.
have	*have*, *has*	had
	Have I got time? Yes, you *have*.	I *had* a good time.
	Has he *got* a mobile phone? Yes, he *has*.	He *had* a late lunch.

Verb	Past Simple
begin	began
break	broke
buy	bought
can	could
come	came
do	did
drink	drank
eat	ate
find	found
get	got
give	gave
go	went
have	had
hear	heard

know	knew
learn	learnt
leave	left
make	made
meet	met
read	read
say	said
see	saw
send	sent
sit	sat
sleep	slept
speak	spoke
take	took
tell	told
write	wrote

OXFORD
UNIVERSITY PRESS

Great Clarendon Street, Oxford, OX2 6DP, United Kingdom

Oxford University Press is a department of the University of Oxford.
It furthers the University's objective of excellence in research, scholarship,
and education by publishing worldwide. Oxford is a registered trade
mark of Oxford University Press in the UK and in certain other countries

ISBN: 978 0 19 457667 3

Printed in China

This book is printed on paper from certified and well-managed sources